Haunted Places of Devon

Rupert Matthews

COUNTRYSIDE BOOKS
NEWBURY BERKSHIRE

·Contents·

Haunted Places of Devon

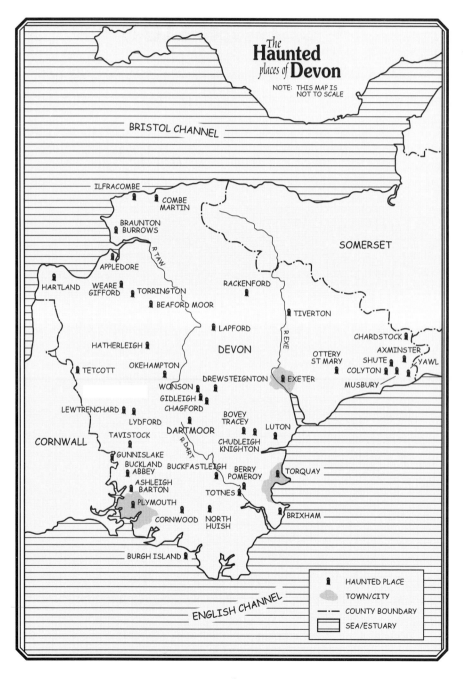

The Haunted *places of* Devon

NOTE: THIS MAP IS NOT TO SCALE

BRISTOL CHANNEL

ILFRACOMBE
COMBE MARTIN
BRAUNTON BURROWS
SOMERSET
R TAW
APPLEDORE
HARTLAND
WEARE GIFFORD
TORRINGTON
RACKENFORD
BEAFORD MOOR
TIVERTON
LAPFORD
CHARDSTOCK
HATHERLEIGH
DEVON
R EXE
OTTERY ST MARY
AXMINSTER
SHUTE
YAWL
TETCOTT
OKEHAMPTON
DREWSTEIGNTON
EXETER
COLYTON
MUSBURY
WONSON
GIDLEIGH
CHAGFORD
LEWTRENCHARD
LYDFORD
BOVEY TRACEY
LUTON
CORNWALL
TAVISTOCK
DARTMOOR
R DART
CHUDLEIGH KNIGHTON
GUNNISLAKE
BUCKLAND ABBEY
BUCKFASTLEIGH
BERRY POMEROY
TORQUAY
ASHLEIGH BARTON
TOTNES
PLYMOUTH
CORNWOOD
NORTH HUISH
BRIXHAM
BURGH ISLAND

ENGLISH CHANNEL

🪦	HAUNTED PLACE
🟣	TOWN/CITY
·-·-	COUNTY BOUNDARY
▭	SEA/ESTUARY

4

• Introduction •

I f there is one county in England famous for its scenic beauty, it is Devon. There are high, wild moorlands and deep, cosy combes. There are bustling towns and quiet villages. Everywhere there is that indefinable something that marks out Devon as one of the most beautiful places in the country.

And everywhere there are ghosts, too.

Some are terrifying, some mundane and a few almost comical. But all of them are part of the history and reality of Devon. As might be expected from a maritime county, the sea and seamen play a large role in the county's phantom legacy. Sir Francis Drake himself strides across the landscape in as dominating a fashion as he did four centuries ago when he was alive. His ghost has been seen on Plymouth Hoe where he played his famous game of bowls and in a pub in Exeter where he used to drink. And his sailors contribute to the ghostly scene of Devon, as do the sweethearts they left behind when they sailed the oceans of the world to fight the Spanish.

There are other ghostly sailors here, too, including the enigmatic man in the white hat at Appledore. There are also plenty of land-based ghosts. Some are as perfectly respectable as the lady of the manor who still visits the village of Lewtrenchard centuries after her death. But others derive from impenetrable mysteries, such as that which overwhelmed a young man just outside Paignton.

What links all these stories, and so many others in this book, is the perfectly natural way in which the witnesses accept the ghosts for what they are. Of course, ghosts are a mystery – we don't know for certain why they appear or why they favour particular places but on the everyday level in which they operate and in which people see them, ghosts can seem almost ordinary.

While researching this book, I visited many haunted sites and spoke to several people who were familiar with the ghosts: 'Oh, you've come about our old man, then' was one response I received when I explained who I was. 'You'd best be talking to Tom,' was another, 'he saw our ghost just last week.'

So, the ghosts and phantoms of Devon are a natural and accepted part of the county life. In this book you will find some of the more famous, as well as those not so well known. In your travels around this wonderful county you may even encounter some of them yourself. Just ask the locals - the chances are that one of Devon's phantoms lurks somewhere nearby.

Rupert Matthews

ILFRACOMBE

Ilfracombe was the first Devon town to become a holiday resort. Its economy boomed when the numerous small beaches, protected by rocky headlands and overlooked by steep hills, were discovered by early 19th century gentry from Devon, keen to emulate the fashionable sea bathing popularised by the Prince Regent in Brighton. The picturesque streets of Ilfracombe down near the old fishing harbour are haunted by two young children dressed in the finest silks

Chambercombe Manor, just outside Ilfracombe, hides secrets as well as phantoms.

7

cut to the fashion of the 17th century. These children come out to play on sunny days, scampering about and laughing. Sadly their history is not so carefree as their phantoms might suggest. The children inherited a small fortune when their parents died and were sent to live with an uncle in Ilfracombe. Only a few weeks after they arrived, the children died of an unexplained disease and the uncle inherited the money. It was widely believed the children had been murdered, but no proof could be found.

To the south-east of the town, a pleasant suburban road gives access to the ancient Chambercombe Manor. The manor house was built in a bad year for England: 1066, the year that William the Conqueror imposed Norman rule. Like many estates, Chambercombe was seized from its English owners and bestowed on a Norman, Sir Henry de Champernowne, whose descendants held the manor for four centuries before it passed to the Greys of Suffolk. Most of the present building was erected by the Greys to serve as a comfortable lodging when they visited their Devon estates.

Among those who spent time there was young Jane Grey. She went to Chambercombe as a teenager, in the early 1550s, when she was becoming famous not just for her beauty but also for her ability to write and speak Greek, Latin, French, Hebrew, and Italian. As a grand-daughter of King Henry VII, Lady Jane Grey unexpectedly found herself hurled into national politics in the summer of 1553. King Edward VI lay dying and there was no generally accepted heir to the throne. The Catholics despised Edward's sister Elizabeth for her Protestant faith, while the Protestants detested his other sister, Mary, for her Catholicism. Both girls had been declared illegitimate by their father, Henry VIII. The powerful Dudley family, which was linked to the Grey's by marriage, put forward young Jane as a compromise candidate.

After Edward's death, she was declared Queen of England on 10th July 1553. However, Mary moved quickly to rally her supporters, and by 20th July she had possession of both London and 'Queen' Jane, whom she promptly put under house arrest. Jane thankfully relinquished the crown and returned to her studies. Sadly, an uprising of Protestant noblemen declared their support for Jane. After the rising was put down, Mary ordered the execution of Lady Jane Grey, who was beheaded at the Tower of London on 12th February 1554.

Soon after the grim scene in London, Lady Jane's ghost began to be seen at Chambercombe. She favoured the grounds over the house, wandering quietly along the paths and among the flowers that she had known for a few brief happy months when she was alive. She was seen in the summer of 2003 by a visitor who described her as wearing a long brown dress and having large expressive eyes that seemed to convey a feeling of weary sadness.

Although the most famous phantom of Chambercombe, Lady Jane Grey is not the only ghost to be seen at this ancient manor. There are two little girls who appear infrequently on the ground floor of the house. The two phantoms do not seem to be connected, as they are not seen together. While one wears Victorian clothes, the other seems to be much older, wearing a plain black dress of the style preferred by Puritans in the 17th century.

Rather more sinister was a discovery made in 1865 in the course of extensive repair and redecoration work. When stripping out some interior woodwork, the tenant discovered a long-hidden interior door. On breaking it down, the man found himself in a small chamber hidden in what he had always thought to be a thick supporting interior wall. Crammed into the room was a bed, on which lay a mouldering skeleton. The bones had obviously been there many years, and, with little chance of discovering the story behind them, the tenant simply called in the local vicar. The bones were wrapped up with care and given a decent, if inexpensive, Christian burial in an unmarked grave at Ilfracombe.

Soon after this grim discovery, disturbances began to happen in the rooms on each side of the newly discovered chamber. The sounds of footsteps echoed when nobody was moving about, and a clearly audible sigh was heard more than once. Then the ghost began to be seen. Like the skeleton, she was tall, and she moved with an elegant step. Those who have seen her say that she is usually smiling faintly as if at a half-forgotten joke.

Of course, stories have grown up around the hidden room and its grim contents. According to one story, the mystery body belonged to a Spanish noblewoman whose ship was wrecked on the nearby coast. The bedraggled survivor was brought to Chambercombe to recover, but died. The owners of the house helped themselves to her jewels and put about the story that she had recovered and gone back to Spain. Another story claims the mystery body was that of the daughter of the house, who discovered that her father was a smuggler or a wrecker and planned to betray him to the law. Rather than face prison, the man murdered his daughter and walled up her body. Such stories are sometimes repeated as if true, but the body remains unidentified and probably its mystery will never be solved – unless the grey lady herself decides to speak out.

COMBE MARTIN

Lying nestled in a steep valley, or combe, that runs down to the sea, Combe Martin is a tranquil spot with a peaceful calm rarely spoiled even in the summer season, when families flock here to enjoy the sandy beach. There are, however, a number of phantoms to enliven the serenity.

One of these ghosts was seen only once, but in most spectacular fashion. In the mid-19th century Squire Ustick of nearby Brynsworthy Manor died after a blameless and merry life, and his body was brought to Combe Martin church for burial. While most of the villagers were inside the church attending the funeral, a few others went about their daily business. They were amazed to see the good squire walking away from the church towards his old home. There the housekeeper saw him enter the house, stride to his favourite armchair in the drawing room, and sit down with a contented smile on his face and a glass of wine in his hand. Then he simply faded from view.

Seen almost as rarely is the phantom bishop who appears at the church. The best report of this ghost was made in 1921, when an observant visitor wrote down details of the sighting just minutes after it happened. The bishop, she recorded, wore a mitre and a cream and gold cloak, which dropped to the floor. Behind him she saw about half a dozen priests in black, and a group of men and women. The observer, a tourist, thought that she was witnessing some quaint re-enactment put on by the villagers for the benefit of visitors such as herself. But then the apparently solid figures faded silently from view. The bishop has been seen since, but not the rest of the phantom procession.

Interestingly, the church contains an elaborate bishop's throne next to the

The ominously named lane that leads up to a haunted hill above Combe Martin.

altar. It was carved in oak sometime in the 14th century. Perhaps the chair was created for a formal visit by the local bishop, an event that is now recreated in spectral form. The rest of the church dates back to 1190, though it was largely rebuilt in the 15th century.

The lane outside the church runs down to the beach, and it is here that the ghostly fiddler is likely to be encountered. He is a cheerful soul, who sits beside the road playing away on his instrument. This man is no great musician, but a typical example of the sort of player who was hired to perform at local weddings, dances, and other celebrations. As might be expected his repertoire is distinctly rustic, being limited to lively dance tunes and folk songs.

Much more grim is the ghost that lurks atop Little Hangman Hill, on the opposite side of the valley from the church. It might be thought that this hill was formerly the site of a gibbet for the execution of local criminals, but this is not the case. The ominous name comes from an incident in the 17th century, when a sheep thief was at work among a flock on this hillside. He used the old trick of identifying the flock's leader, throwing a rope around her neck, and dragging her off, the rest of the flock would be sure to follow. On this particular night, the thief tumbled down the cliffs, the rope getting caught around his neck as he fell. The sheep at the other end of the rope got caught in bushes, and the unfortunate man was found dead, hanging by his neck, the next morning. Given his dishonest way of life, it is unlikely the man was much mourned by the good folk of Combe Martin.

BRAUNTON BURROWS

The coast north of the Taw Estuary is marked by extensive beaches and towering sand dunes, built up by the wind and waves. Many years ago this stretch of coast was among the various Devon estates of the hot-headed and ambitious young knight William de Tracy. One fateful day in 1170, young William and three friends were at the court of King Henry II, when they heard the king raging against the intransigence of the Archbishop of Canterbury, Thomas à Becket. 'Will no-one rid me of this turbulent priest?,' shouted the king at his cowed court. De Tracy and his friends took the king at his word. They rode to Canterbury and slew the archbishop.

The king at once repented of his hasty words, but this did nothing to calm the anger of the Church or of the people. Penances were imposed on King Henry and the four knights. Although de Tracy worked out his penances before he died, the good folk of Devon never forgave him for this act. It is said that his ghost is condemned to exist on windswept Braunton Burrows. There he must twist the sand into rope to gain his entry into Heaven. As if that task were not quite impossible, it is said that the sands are patrolled by a great black dog raised from Hell itself and that, if the ghostly Sir William ever looks like completing his task, the dog breathes out a ball of fire which destroys his work. The ghost of Sir William de Tracy is also seen at Lapford.

APPLEDORE

At Appledore the estuaries of the Taw and Torridge merge before flowing out into the Bristol Channel. Even today, with the modern bridges, the route round to Wrafton, on the north shore, is a long one. In days gone by, the walk around the estuaries by way of Bideford and Barnstaple could take all day, and it is no wonder that local people tended to travel by boat as much as by road.

One such voyager returns time and again to the waterfront at Appledore. He wears a white hat and calls out to passing boats, asking for a trip across the waters to Wrafton. Some boatmen who have seen the phantom man report that he seems quite distressed, as if getting to Wrafton is a matter of great urgency for him. In the years before the Second World War, he was seen so often that he became something of a local joke, and was called Old White Hat by the sailors. He has never told anyone why he wants a lift, however. If a boat puts in to help him, the ghost vanishes abruptly.

The shoreline at Appledore, where sailors have reported a strange spectre in a white hat.

Just up a narrow lane from the quayside stands the Bell Inn. This ancient pub is haunted by no less than three ghosts. The best known is a phantom sailor, who wears a flamboyant three-cornered hat. He walks in from the street to enter the bar, starts across the room, and then just vanishes. He was seen in March 2004 by an American visitor. Thinking the strangely dressed newcomer might be a local in fancy dress, the visitor approached him – and shook with fright when he walked straight through her outstretched arm. Seen rather less often is the man upstairs. He walks onto the first floor landing through a solid brick wall. This wall formerly gave access to a neighbouring cottage, which was pulled down over 40 years ago. Presumably this man in Victorian clothes is simply carrying on as if the cottage and connecting door still existed. Rather more enigmatic is the woman who appears only after dark. She is seen infrequently, but is sensed rather more often. She is a friendly, watchful spirit who enters the bedroom of sleeping guests to bend over them. Lulu, the landlady in 2004, reported that the woman behaves just as a mother does when bending over a baby's cot. She creeps gently across the room to look down on the sleeper and listen carefully to their breathing. Assured that all is well, she then vanishes from view.

The Bell Inn at Appledore is home to three ghosts.

Hartland Abbey and the fields where the ghostly monks are seen.

HARTLAND

The village of Hartland was once the largest and most prosperous town in the area. It had a market, a mayor, and a charter. Such bustling days faded centuries ago, and Hartland is now a typically rural north Devon village.

The ghosts of Hartland are not to be found in the village itself, but round and about. The road to the east of the village is haunted by a mounted man wearing a large hat with a wide brim. He is usually described as being quite friendly, waving at fellow riders or pedestrians, but steadfastly ignoring motorists.

The road north-west of the village runs down towards scenic Hartland Point, one of the most ruggedly romantic stretches of coastline in Devon. Just before the coast the road passes Hartland Abbey. This is now a magnificent pseudo-Gothic stately home, but in medieval times was a prosperous monastery. The ruins of the monastic buildings can be found in the grounds of the mansion. A procession of half a dozen phantom monks will sometimes form up among the ruins, cross the meadows, and set off along the road towards Hartland.

A little over a mile west of Hartland stands the parish church dedicated to St Nectan. This Welsh priest came to Cornwall to preach Christianity in the dying days of the Roman Empire, moving to Devon as he grew older. It is said that when an old man, St Nectan was attacked on the road at Newton Cross by pagan brigands, who sliced off his head. Miraculously, St Nectan picked up his head and staggered home to his cell near Hartland, where he finally expired. The present church was built much later, but occupies the spot where he was buried. His ghost has been seen several times in and around the church. He wears a simple brown garment, rather like a long smock, with a belt around the waist. He walks with a stoop, as if worn down by the cares of the years.

WEARE GIFFORD

A short way downstream of Torrington, the River Torridge winds across wide meadows, which flood frequently after rain, and then skirts the little village of Weare Gifford. The road from Torrington crosses the river, and then runs across the flood meadows before reaching the ancient church, built safe and dry on a small rise in the land.

It is along this damp stretch of road that the sad spectre of Louise Dillon has been seen. This unfortunate young woman was murdered here by her farmer husband in May 1887. The cause of the violent quarrel, witnessed by several villagers, was never established. Within minutes of the killing, the husband, William Dillon, slit his own throat. The soft outline of the woman has been seen walking along the fateful road towards their cottage home.

The church of the Holy Trinity at Weare Gifford.

In a contrasting story of a happy marriage, the churchyard and church are haunted by a venerable phantom, who has walked here since 1243. Sir Walter Gifford died away from home and so was not buried in the church, alongside his wife, Alice, as he had wished. On still, moonlit nights, the ghost of Sir Walter walks from his old home, Weare Gifford Hall, to enter the churchyard and stroll up the footpath to the church door. There he pauses, knocks once, and waits. The door opens of its own accord, and Sir Walter enters. Presumably he is seeking his beloved wife. That, at least, is the story. It is odd, therefore, that the tombs of both Sir Walter and Lady Alice lie in the nave of the church. Perhaps that of Sir Walter lacks a body, having been prepared in advance.

TORRINGTON

The small town of Great Torrington, known locally simply as Torrington, stands on a magnificent site. It is perched on a steep hill high above the River Torridge and offers magnificent views across the rolling North Devon countryside.

The town had spent the centuries mostly in the quiet guise of a market town, where the farmers of the surrounding rich lands came to sell their produce, buy tools, and gossip with each other, but on 9th February 1646 everything changed.

On that day an army of 4,000 cavalry and 3,000 infantry marched into Torrington. At their head rode Prince Charles, later to be King Charles II. Because the prince, young, dashing and handsome was just 15 and leading his first army, the command was really in the hands of the veteran Lord Ralph Hopton.

This small army was the last hope of the Royalists in the Civil War that had broken out in 1642. The cities of Chester, Exeter, Oxford, and Newark held for the king, as did fortresses dotted throughout the kingdom, but the main Royalist army had been destroyed at the battle of Naseby. Not only was Hopton's army the only force loyal to the king left in the field, but it guarded stocks of food and ammunition that were King Charles's only remaining supplies. The king had no money left and could afford no more.

Hopton was hoping to move his army south to break the siege of Exeter, and had chosen hilltop Torrington as a fortified supply dump. His first move, therefore, was to erect barricades and fortifications around the town. Six days later a scout brought in the unwelcome news that Sir Thomas Fairfax, the Parliamentarian commander, had led his army away from Exeter and was now marching on Torrington. Even worse, reinforcements under Oliver Cromwell had joined Fairfax, who now had 12,000 men with him. Ominously for Hopton, most of these men were hardened veterans, while his own forces were largely new recruits from Cornwall and Devon.

Hopton sent his few experienced cavalry forward to harry the Parliamentarian scouts and slow their advance. On 16th February Fairfax sent

his men to attack the Royalist defences at Torrington. It had been raining almost constantly for a week and the ground was a muddy quagmire, but the sun shone that Saturday morning and the temperature was unseasonably warm. The Royalists fought well throughout the day and into the night. Only when Fairfax sent in his reserves did the defences fail. First to go was the barricade in Well Street, but once the Parliamentarians were in the town, Hopton ordered his entire army to pull out. Using his veteran cavalry as an effective rearguard, Hopton sent Prince Charles racing ahead to safety. Meanwhile he defended the swollen River Torridge until most of his army had disappeared into the winter night.

Back in Torrington, some 50 Royalist prisoners had been herded into the church, and the doors locked, while the Parliamentarians searched the town for fugitives and wounded. Fairfax and Cromwell were standing in the market place issuing orders, when the night was torn apart by an enormous explosion. A vast ball of orange fire lifted the roof off the church, blew out the windows, and scattered masonry in all directions. Cromwell escaped unharmed, but Fairfax was thrown to the ground and a horse beside him was killed by the blast. The Royalist store of gunpowder, kept in the church vaults, had exploded. Fairfax later wrote: 'The prisoners and our men that guarded them were killed and overwhelmed in the ruines, the houses of the town shaken and shattered and our men all the town over much endangered by the stones, timber and lead which with the blast were carried up very high and scattered in great abundance all the town over and beyond. Yet it pleased God that very few of our men were slain or hurt thereby.'

A week later, the Roundheads marched out of the shattered town of Torrington to pursue Hopton. The Royalists, now lacking supplies and ammunition, could not hope to face Fairfax in open battle. After some weeks of fruitless manoeuvring, Hopton surrendered. Prince Charles escaped to fight another day, but the royalist cause was effectively dead. The battle of Torrington had secured England for Parliament.

The citizens of Torrington spent many months clearing up. The great blast of gunpowder had not only destroyed the church, leaving just the walls standing, but had also blown out nearly every window in the town and had stripped the roofs off dozens of houses. By the autumn the town was largely repaired, but the phantom marks of the fateful day remain.

Unsurprisingly, the most haunted spot is the church and its immediate area. Here, the ghosts of Cavaliers have been seen. They do not appear to be particularly military in bearing, preferring to sit about talking or gently strolling around. Perhaps they prefer to recall happier times before they joined the army of Hopton and marched to their deaths.

The site of the barricade in Well Street is also a focus for hauntings. The ghosts here are heard more often than seen. The sound of marching men, tramping boots, and clanking arms fills the air around dusk. Occasionally, a woman's voice is heard among the sounds of war. Who she was and how she got mixed up in the fighting is unknown.

RACKENFORD

Small and somewhat isolated, Rackenford nevertheless was once a booming market town. In the 1730s, Rackenford attracted visits from a very wealthy young man. From time to time he would ride into the village, secure a room at the Stag Inn and spend his money freely on whatever Rackenford had to offer in the way of food, drink, and entertainments. Having stayed a few weeks, the mysterious stranger would ride off again, only to return

The door to the Stag Inn at Rackenford where the ghost of a notorious highwayman has been seen.

after an absence of some weeks or months.

In February 1735, the elegantly dressed horseman left Rackenford for the last time. Only later, did the villagers discover that their free-spending guest had been none other than the notorious highwayman Tom King. King had been tempted away from his West Country haunts by an offer to team up with the equally notorious Dick Turpin. The two men planned to become rich attacking the wealthy merchants who travelled between London and the provincial cities of York, Norwich, and Bristol. For some months everything went well for the unscrupulous pair, but then they were ambushed by the Bow Street Runners. In the shoot-out that followed, Turpin shot King by mistake and then fled. King died by the roadside.

Then his ghost returned to the Stag Inn in Rackenford. It still appears from time to time, as King did in life, riding his horse into the courtyard and striding into the bar. He has also been seen lurking in the porch, perhaps keeping any eye open for any sign of the forces of law and order.

Rackenford's second ghost is that of the 19th-century vicar Parson Froud. In life, this vicar enjoyed the country pursuits of hunting, shooting, and fishing far more than his religious duties. Perhaps that is why after death he returns in spectral form mounted on his favourite black hunter. His ghost has been seen galloping over the fields around the village and even, on one occasion, in the village itself.

TIVERTON

Tiverton has long been dominated by the castle and church, which stand together on top of the hill above the River Exe. The two buildings are closely connected to the ghost that wanders the streets between and near them. In 1485, the Plantagenet dynasty that ruled England for centuries was brought to a final and bloody end when Richard III was killed at the Battle of Bosworth.

Among the various problems that the new Tudor King Henry VII had to face was what to do with the surviving Plantagenets. Prime among these was Princess Katherine, a niece of the slaughtered Richard. In 1495, the 16 year old Katherine was married off to William Courtney, Earl of Devon. Courtney had fought with Henry at Bosworth and could be relied upon not to use his wife as a lever to power. To make doubly certain, Henry gave the couple a handsome dowry conditional on their staying in Devon. Thus Princess Katherine came to Tiverton Castle. Clearly, she was happy here; she brought up a fine family, and, after her husband died in 1511, rarely left the town and her nearby estates. She endowed the church with a magnificent chapel and when the dowager countess died in 1527, she was buried in an elaborate tomb in her new chapel.

For some time all was peaceful, but in 1645 the English Civil War came to Tiverton. The castle was held for the king, and so the Roundheads, under Thomas Fairfax, brought up their cannon to pound the garrison into submission. The Parliamentarian gunners were clearly not good at aiming, for they managed to destroy Princess Katherine's chapel as well as the castle walls. The tomb was smashed into fragments by the gunfire.

No doubt this is what prompted the departed countess to begin her wanderings. Soon after the Parliamentarian army moved on to Great Torrington, the ghost of a woman dressed in the fashion of a century earlier began to be seen around the church. She has not ceased her walking since. Perhaps poor Princess Katherine is seeking her scattered bones and lost tomb.

•The East•

CHARDSTOCK

T he village of Chardstock is mentioned in Domesday Book as being rich enough to maintain two knights to serve in the army when required; so it must have been a fairly substantial place. It was owned by the Bishop of Salisbury, and by 1377 it had a fine church.

By the mid-19th century, however, the church at Chardstock was in poor

The haunted lane at Chardstock.

condition. The roof leaked, the walls needed repair, and the windows let in the wind. The chancel remained upright thanks only to the stout metal bars that propped it up. Many other villages may have contented themselves with repairs and renovations, but Chardstock had as its vicar the Revd Charles Woodcock, who had inherited enormous wealth from his father, a merchant with the East India Company in Madras.

In 1861, Woodcock ordered that the entire church be pulled down and completely rebuilt. The work was finished in time for the Bishop of Salisbury to consecrate the new church in 1864. The good vicar went on to build a new vicarage and new village schools, which, like the church, have barely been altered since. Woodcock served as vicar for 40 years, staying in the village after he retired and dying there in 1898.

Nevertheless it is not the devoted Revd Woodcock who haunts the church and vicarage, but his wife. This woman was every bit as energetic as her husband, founding societies for the local women, as well as devoting much time to the schools. She is seen hurrying up the lane from the vicarage to the church. For some reason she seems to prefer to walk at dusk, scurrying through the gathering gloom on some long-forgotten task of great urgency.

AXMINSTER

The best known phantom of the town of Axminster, famous for its carpets, is no longer to be seen. This was the spectre of a Jewish pedlar who was murdered in the Dolphin Inn during the 17th century. He was seen frequently in the old pub, but it has now been demolished and the ghost walks no longer.

Another phantom that has not been seen for years is the ghost coach that formerly pulled out of the town on the road towards Honiton. It used to be seen quite regularly and was featured in the local press, but has not put in an appearance for at least 30 years.

Rather more enduring are the ghosts of Warlake Hill, just outside the town. This hill was the scene of a terrible battle many centuries ago when the Angles,

Saxons, and Jutes began to invade the Britain deserted by the Romans, driving the Britons to the outer margins. The battle fought here resulted in a great victory for the invaders and utter ruin for the Britons. Eventually, the Britons from this area were driven west of the Tamar river, where they survived as the Cornish.

It is said that five kings were killed in the battle on Warlake Hill and were buried where they fell. Their spirits are clearly not at rest. On cloudless nights when a waxing moon bathes the landscape with its pale light, the five kings rise from their graves. The ghostly royal warriors walk the field of battle, waving their weapons and shouting their warcries; then they drift back to their graves and sink down into the ground.

SHUTE

The lane leading into the village of Shute is flanked by two mysterious pillars built of stone and topped by ornamental balls. These have stood here for longer than anyone can remember. They are generally thought to be connected to the old medieval manor of Shute Barton, but nobody is entirely certain.

What is known for certain is that the ghost that lurks here is linked to Shute House. Back in 1787, this grand house was owned by Sir John Pole, a man blessed with a sizeable fortune, a strapping son, and pair of pretty daughters. One of these girls fell in love with the handsome coachman who drove the family around on social visits and business. Sir John, not wanting his daughter to marry beneath her, sacked the man and forbade his daughter to see him again.

Some weeks later, Sir John's son caught the young lovers in each other's arms enjoying a kiss behind one of the Shute pillars. Grabbing the whip from his carriage, the son laid into the coachman and gave the poor man such a horsewhipping that he died. Ever since then, the figure of the handsome young man has been seen ducking and diving and twisting from side to side as if trying to evade the lashing of some invisible whip.

YAWL

The road that runs from Yawl to Uplyme, near the borders with Dorset, is haunted by the leader of a doomed rebellion. This road, now designated the A3070, leads inland from the port of Lyme Regis. In the summer of 1683, the Duke of Monmouth landed at Lyme Regis to raise the standard of Protestant revolt against the Catholic king – his own uncle, James II. Monmouth was the illegitimate son of the previous king, Charles II, but claimed his father had married his mother in secret, which made him the rightful king of England. Dorset, Devon, and Somerset rose to support Monmouth, but, before his rebellion could gather much momentum, Monmouth and his farmboys were caught at Sedgemoor in Somerset by the professional royal army and destroyed. Monmouth was captured, dragged to

The road at Yawl is haunted by the Duke of Monmouth.

London and beheaded. Ironically, the harsh treatment James handed out to Monmouth and his followers did much to undermine the little support he had. In 1685, James had to flee a second, and better planned, Protestant rebellion that put his own daughter, Mary, on the throne.

The ghost of the Duke of Monmouth, dressed in rich clothes and waving a wide-brimmed hat decorated with feathers canters along the road at Yawl on his great white charger. Poor Monmouth seems to be waving to a cheering crowd, and his route inland was indeed lined with supporters. Presumably he comes back here to relive the happier times before his rebellion went so tragically wrong.

COLYTON

According to the Devon Tourist Office in Plymouth, Colyton is the most haunted village in the county. Whether or not this is strictly true, it certainly does have more than its fair share of phantoms.

The fine house that served for years as the vicarage was built as a manor house for Thomas Brerewode in the reign of Henry VIII. As a staunch Catholic, Brerewode opposed the king's divorce from Katherine of Aragon. He carved a pomegranate on the gates of his house, that fruit being the queen's emblem. Brerewode suffered for his loyalty. He was imprisoned, though briefly, and heavily fined. It is said that he hid the family silver somewhere in Colyton to stop it falling into the hands of the king's agents. His ghost has been seen lurking near his old home, and local belief has it that he is searching for his lost treasure.

The church at Colyton is famous for its oddly-shaped tower. The churchyard is haunted by a woman in grey, said to turn her head away from anyone who sees her. Whether this is from modesty or shame is as unknown, as is her history.

Down by the river are spreading water meadows, which flood easily after heavy rain. This area is the haunt of a young woman who is said by all who see her to be quite startlingly attractive. The girl walks slowly along the banks of the river, gazing thoughtfully into the waters. Quite who this pretty girl might

The stone seat overlooking Colyton, which is still haunted by the gentle vicar who had it built.

be is not known. She wears a loose-flowing dress that might date from almost any period of history. Some believe that she may not be a human ghost at all, but rather the ancient pagan spirit of the waters, who was worshiped as a goddess here in Roman times.

High above the village, at the top of a hill near the end of Hillhead Lane, there is a stone bench. This was erected by the vicar, the Revd Roderick Barnes, in the 1830s. Barnes held the living here from 1807 to 1860 and his daily walk took him to the top of this hill to enjoy the stunning views. He put the bench there to give himself somewhere to rest before starting off back down the hill to the village. His ghost has been seen sitting on the bench and enjoying the views many times since his death.

MUSBURY

The church of St Michael at Musbury has stood here for centuries. There was a chapel here before the Norman conquest, though the oldest part of the present church is the tower, which was erected in around 1420; the rest was erected during the following 100 years or so.

There is an old tunnel, now fallen in, that links the church to Ashe House. It was in this manor house that John Churchill, later to be the great Duke of Marlborough, was born in 1650, though the ghost of Musbury has nothing to do with the Churchills, but with the family who owned the manor before them. In 1549 it was bought by John Drake. At this time the Drakes were a farming family, of which John was the leading member. Some years later, an impecunious cousin, Francis Drake, won fame and fortune raiding the treasure galleons of England's enemy, Spain.

In 1577 word reached Musbury that Francis Drake was recruiting men for a new voyage. A young man of Musbury, named Bernard, was in love with a local girl, but the girl's farmer father had forbidden a marriage, as Bernard was too poor. Desperate to marry his love, Bernard volunteered to join the voyage and win his fortune. The girl, her name is not recorded, promised to wait for his return.

A year after Drake's fleet of five ships set out, two of them returned to Plymouth. They reported that the fleet had explored much of the east coast of South America, but then a mighty storm had arisen. One of the ships was seen to sink, and the other two had vanished into the storm. Poor Bernard was aboard one of these ships, as was Drake himself. The months passed with no news of Drake or his lost ships. It was widely believed he must have sunk or been cast ashore in wild, unexplored terrain.

In Musbury, the girl still waited. As she was both pretty and stood to inherit her father's farm, she was not short of admirers. Finally, in the spring of 1580, she accepted that her Bernard must be dead and agreed to marry the son of a farmer from nearby Kilmington. The wedding was set for Midsummer's Day. The day of the wedding came, and the two families, together with most of the

The porch of Musbury church, out of which no less than six phantoms walk in silent procession.

population of Musbury, gathered in the church of St Michael. The bride arrived, decked in her wedding finery and walked demurely up the aisle to the altar. Suddenly a window was shattered to a thousand fragments by a deafening crash. A great iron cannonball slammed into the floor of the church and rumbled slowly across the flagstones. It came to a rest at the foot of the bride, who promptly fainted.

It could mean only one thing. Bernard was still alive. Somehow, it was believed, he had heard of the wedding and sent a cannonball flying from his distant ship. After all, the villagers muttered, it was well known that Francis Drake was in league with the Devil. The vicar ordered the window to be blocked up as it had been touched by the Devil's work, and it remains blocked to this day.

On 26th September Drake in his ship, *Golden Hind*, sailed into Plymouth Sound. His voyage had taken him right around the world and brought him a vast treasure in looted Spanish gold and valuable spices. Young Bernard returned to Musbury in triumph and wealthier than any man in the village. He married his love before Christmas and together they lived a long and happy life.

It is generally thought that it must be this nameless girl who is the ghost that walks quietly around the churchyard. She has long dark hair neatly tucked beneath a bonnet and walks with leisurely steps.

Part of the vast new-found wealth of the Drake family found its way to the Drakes of Musbury. They spent some of it on a grand tomb in 1611 and more when the tomb was extended in 1646. On the tomb kneel life-sized effigies of three generations of the Drake family. It is firmly believed in the village that at midnight on nights of the full moon these stone carvings come to life. They leave the church and walk down to the stream. There they bend to drink, before returning to their rightful places in the church.

OTTERY ST MARY

The little town of Ottery St Mary is best known for its magnificent church, founded in 1337 as the centrepiece of a religious college that trained priests, monks, lay clerics, and choristers. This huge building is much larger than the needs of such a town could ever have warranted and was built as a scaled down copy of Exeter cathedral.

When the Reformation swept England, the foundation at Ottery St Mary was closed down, but the church survived, as the town took it over as its own parish church. Among the few interior treasures to survive the Reformation is the astronomical clock. Installed in the south transept when the church was built, this instrument shows the phases of the moon and the date as well as the time.

Across the nave from the clock stands the magnificent tomb of John Coke. The Cokes were the great landowners around Ottery St Mary during the 17th century, and John was both a wealthy landowner and noted soldier. He chose to commission a tomb that shows him standing upright, dressed in the armour that served him so well as a soldier. Unfortunately, the armour did not save him from being stabbed in the back, quite literally, by his own brother during a family quarrel over the estates. He died on 28th March 1632, and every year on the anniversary of his death, the fine effigy climbs down from the tomb and walks round the church. It then leaves by the north porch and walks three times around the churchyard. Satisfied that his wicked brother is not buried in the holy grounds of the church of St Mary, John Coke returns to his tomb.

EXETER

The cathedral city of Devon is Exeter, which has been inhabited for at least 2,200 years and possibly longer. Its name means '(Roman) fortified town on the Exe', but none of the numerous phantoms to be encountered in this delightful city is quite as old as its name.

Possibly the most ancient ghost of Exeter is the phantom nun who is seen to wander the old cloisters beside the cathedral on summer evenings. There is some sense of sadness about this phantom. She walks with her head bowed from the north of the cloisters to the south.

Cathedral Close is also haunted by a monk. He is seen only rarely and fleetingly, standing outside house no.5 and slipping from view almost as quickly

Exeter Cathedral has dominated the city centre for centuries and attracts a number of ghosts.

as he appears. Some people think that the two ghosts are linked. It is rumoured that they date from the time of the great rebuilding of the cathedral in the 14th century, when Exeter heaved with workmen, tradesmen, and religious figures of all kinds. John, the monk, and Martha, the nun, had come to Exeter from their respective houses to supervise the more spiritual aspects of the rebuilding. The pair, it is said, fell deeply in love. When the time came for them to return to their secluded houses, they could not bear to be parted and they committed suicide so that they could be together forever.

Sadly, the ghosts are never seen together. The suicide pact does not seem to have worked. Whether the story has any basis in fact is unclear; it was not recorded until centuries after the events are supposed to have taken place.

Rather better documented is the story of the phantom verger, who has been seen inside the cathedral. This man died in the later 19th century and was observed soon after his death fussing around a side chapel as if going about his duties. He has been seen several times since, and more than one person has mistaken him for a real verger and tried to ask a question about the superb cathedral. Unlike most cathedrals, there is no central tower at Exeter, and so the 70 ft high ribbed vaulting of the ceiling runs uninterrupted from end to end of the building to form the longest such stone vault in the world. The twin towers that flank the crossing are the oldest part of the cathedral, dating from Norman times. The rest of the building dates from the 14th century, when a new nave, choir, and chapels were erected as a harmonious whole.

Just down the hill from the cathedral is the White Hart Hotel, which stands on the site of the old south gate in the now largely vanished city wall. The courtyard of this welcoming old inn is haunted by a young woman dressed in black. Those who have seen her say that she wears a flowing black cape or coat that effectively wraps her from neck to toe. She usually appears in the courtyard, walks out into South Street, and then vanishes.

Beyond the White Hart, the lane known as Quay Hill drops down steeply to the river Exe. It opens out into a broad, cobbled street, flanked on one side by the river and on the other by an impressive collection of old buildings. This is Exeter's historic Quayside area. Throughout most of the city's history, ships have been able to get up the Exe, and Exeter has had a busy time as a port. Only

Cathedral Close, Exeter, haunted by several phantoms.

in the later 19th century did ships become too large to get upriver. The Quayside went through a period of neglect, but it has now been handsomely refurbished to house a market, antique stalls, craft workshops, pubs, and restaurants.

The most impressive building of all is the Custom House, which continued to house Her Majesty's Customs and Excise staff until 1989. When this building was erected, it was the largest brick building not just in Exeter but in all Devon. The wide ground floor arches, which now house windows, were originally an open arcade which allowed the customs officials to inspect the wagon loads of goods under cover before they were taken off the dockside. This fact was unknown to the lady who, in the 1980s, saw the Quayside's phantom wagon drive straight through one of the walls and into the Custom House.

The wagon, pulled by two horses and loaded with goods, is not the most active ghostly apparition on the old Quayside. That honour belongs to the

The Ship Inn stands in a narrow lane in central Exeter and is haunted by a Tudor gentleman, said to be none other than Sir Francis Drake.

Victorian girl who haunts The Prospect, the oldest pub on the ancient docks. This little child grasps a rag doll firmly in her arms as she skips playfully around the pub. She seems perfectly happy and no story attaches to her. Who she is and why she haunts The Prospect is unknown.

A fine pair of adjoining buildings in the High Street are said to be haunted, though whether by the same ghost is unclear. The ancient Turk's Head pub has for centuries played host to the ghost of a red-headed woman in a long green dress. She is said to walk slowly round the ground floor, but is never in sight for very long. This ghost has the knack of being seen just as she walks out of sight through a door or behind a post. The Turk's Head shares its cellar with the Guildhall next door. This building too is said to be haunted by a woman. She has not been seen recently, however; so it is difficult to get a good description. Perhaps she is the same woman in green, perhaps not.

Outside in the High Street, however the ghost of the great Victorian novelist Charles Dickens has been seen. Dickens spent a lot of time in Exeter and lodged at the Turk's Head on most visits. He is sometimes spotted standing quietly by the side of the road, watching the passersby intently.

Down an alley off the High Street stands the ancient Ship Inn. The sign outside depicts a 16th century warship surging through a stormy sea under a

A terrifying encounter, which took place on the Honiton Road.

press of canvas. The sign is appropriate, for it was here that Sir Francis Drake lodged when visiting Exeter. The dashing sea rover has been seen several times since his death. He wears a doublet and hose of a most fashionable cut and stalks restlessly through the pub.

During the 1970s the Ship Inn experienced some strange phenomena. A few people found themselves being pushed gently from behind as they walked down the stairs, though nobody was behind them. Various small objects went missing around the pub, only to turn up in unexpected places. At the time the events were linked to the ghost of Drake, but if so he soon tired of his pranks.

Sir Francis Drake was a dominant figure in Devon in the 16th century, and his ghost may be encountered in Plymouth and at Buckland Abbey as well as in Exeter's Ship Inn. And he is linked to another haunting at Musbury.

The area of the city to the north of the Ship Inn was heavily bombed by the Luftwaffe during the Second World War. These attacks not only destroyed many charming streets and historic buildings but also deprived some of Exeter's more active ghosts of a home.

The most famous of these vanished phantoms was Queen Henrietta Maria, the wife of Charles I. During the English Civil War, Queen Henrietta Maria took refuge in the strongly fortified city of Exeter while her husband led the Cavaliers against the Roundheads, who supported Parliament. In June 1644, she gave birth to Princess Henrietta Anne, but just days later was forced to flee to France by the approach of a hostile army. The princess was left behind in Exeter and was baptised in the cathedral amid as much pomp as could be mustered in the circumstances. Neither mother nor daughter saw Charles I again. He was executed by Parliament in 1649. The princess was later shipped off to France to be brought up in somewhat impoverished circumstances by her mother. She later married the brother of the King of France, but the marriage was unhappy and she died, allegedly of poison, in 1670. The ghost of the royal mother cradling her baby was a frequent sight in the house where she lodged during her time in Exeter. The house has gone now, and so has her ghost.

Another spectre no longer to be seen is that of Elliot Drake, who lived at Nutwell Court on the road to Exmouth a generation or two after his illustrious relative, Sir Francis. Wild and impetuous, young Elliot was drinking one night in Exeter when the talk turned to the merits of the horses owned by the various young gallants around the table. Elliot challenged those present to a race back to Nutwell Court. The race took a tragic turn when Elliot was thrown by his horse at the very gates of his home and the poor man broke his neck. The ghost of Elliot was seen several times recreating his last ride at full gallop. The ghost, unlike the man, reached home and dismounted before vanishing. The ghost has not been seen for at least 25 years, the current owners of Nutwell Court have lived there since 1977 and have so far seen nothing.

The road from Exeter to Honiton, now the A30, was also the scene of a dramatic haunting. The ghost concerned was seen just once in the late 19th century. Two sailors on leave from Plymouth were walking east along the road towards their homes. At some point outside Exeter – they did not record where – they were confronted by the apparition of the drummer boy who served with the marines on board their ship. The figure had a deep gash across his forehead. Convinced that something was very wrong, the two men turned round and hurried back to their ship in Plymouth. They found the boy had been murdered by one of the sailors. Why the ghost had appeared to the two sailors is a mystery, for the returning men played no part in catching the killer, though they did stay to watch him hang.

Drewsteignton

At the heart of this hilltop village is the square, with the impressive church on one side and a welcoming pub on another. This is clearly a village where the womenfolk are a redoubtable lot; in the last century the pub had a landlady who managed the business with efficient charm for no less than 70 years.

Just as impressive is the feat reputedly carried out by three spinsters from Drewsteignton one morning many years ago. The three sisters awoke this particular morning but, for some reason, did not feel up to eating their usual fried breakfast of impressively large size. So, in order to work up an appetite, they went for a stroll down the hill. There they came across four boulders, which they playfully tossed about. Eventually, tiring of their game, the girls placed three of the stones upright and balanced the fourth across the top. Now suitably in need of nourishment, they trotted back up the hill to tuck into their sausages, bacon and eggs.

The Spinsters' Rocks still stand where they left them. These must have been strong girls. The upright stones stand over six feet tall, while the slab across the top measures about fourteen feet in length. In reality, of course, this is a prehistoric tomb. Originally, there would have been a mound of earth over the stones, but this has worn away in the course of the past 4,500 years. There is no doubt, however, that women are connected to the stones in some way, for

The ancient Spinsters' Rocks, allegedly built one morning by three sisters from Drewsteignton.

the faintly outlined shape of a woman in a long cloak has been seen here in the early morning. Perhaps it is the ghost of a prehistoric noblewoman who was buried here.

The village of Drewsteignton itself was formerly famous for an indelible bloodstain on the pavement outside the house where a foul murder was committed in the 18th century and the blood came leaking out from under the front door. It was said that on the anniversary of the crime each year, the stain became wet and the pavement once again ran red with blood. However, in 2004 the stain could not be found, though several local people knew of the story.

Just below the village, the River Teign runs through a narrow gorge, which is famous for its trout fishing. In the midst of the quiet ravine lie the still, dark waters of Bradford Pool. It is here that a ferocious ghost lurks, which claims the life of one person each year. Some believe that talk of this ghost is merely a way to dissuade the local children from swimming in the fast-flowing river, which can be treacherous after heavy rain. Others believe that the ghost, if it is there, is the last surviving manifestation of a pagan water god, to which human sacrifice was once made.

To be on the safe side, though, it is probably best to keep to the dry riverside paths when visiting the gorge.

BOVEY TRACEY

There are two quite different hauntings at Bovey Tracey: one very public, and the other intensely private. The first takes place on the bridge over the river Bovey in the heart of the village. The phantom

The old bridge at Bovey Tracey where a woman in a long coat appears with much frequency.

seen here is of a young woman dressed in a long coat, some say a raincoat. She appears at night, usually quite late. This phantom is seen only by drivers and passengers in cars and trucks that pass over the bridge. She comes from nowhere and rushes out into the path of the vehicle. Waving her arms frantically, the woman clearly wants the driver to stop and sometimes even hurls herself at the vehicle. Whether the driver stops in time to avoid a collision with the ghost or not, the aftermath is always the same. The road is empty and no woman is in sight. It is usually assumed that the woman was the victim of some accident on this spot in the past, but there are no records of a young woman being killed here. The mystery remains.

The more private phantom of Bovey Tracey is a monk. At least, he is assumed to be a monk. One of the older houses in the village has a staircase that came from the old Buckfast Abbey. A heavy male is heard climbing the stairs from time to time, but no figure is ever seen. The phantom seems a gentle soul who causes neither anxiety nor distress.

CHUDLEIGH KNIGHTON

This apparently serene little village has a great reputation for being haunted, but the stories vary as to exactly what it is that lurks here. It is the bridge over the river Teign, just outside the village, that is the centre of the hauntings. This bridge has long been said to be beloved by the Devil. He is alleged to wait here for unwary travellers, or those whose souls are deeply mired by sin, and then he will pounce. Most people thought this gossip was little more than a harmless tale until the night of 8th February 1855. That night the Devil came to Chudleigh Knighton.

The winter of 1854–55 was unusually severe. Deep snow lay across Devon for weeks on end and a particularly heavy fall came on 8th February. Few people were about that day, and those that were hurried to be home before dark. Just around midnight that night the dogs of Chudleigh Knighton began to bark and howl. Dogs in other villages soon joined in.

Next day, the good folk of Chudleigh Knighton emerged to find a strange

High Street, Chudleigh Knighton, close to the ancient bridge where a deformed dwarf lurks at night.

set of footprints leading from under the haunted bridge over the Teign. The footprints were those of a hoofed animal that walked upright on two legs. Each of the hoofprints was about two and a half inches across and they were spaced eight inches apart. Without doubt these were the footprints of the Devil. The tracks left the bridge and moved through the village. In places, it seemed the evil visitor had approached the doors of some houses, paused awhile, and then left. They gave the church a wide berth, and then headed south towards Bishopsteignton. A few villagers, braver than the rest, followed the prints. They found the people of Bishopsteignton as worried by the hoofprints as they were themselves. Even more perplexing, the days that followed revealed that the hoofprints had also been found across other large areas of southern Devon.

From Bishopsteignton the tracks led east to Teignmouth and then north to Dawlish, Starcross, and Powderham. They crossed the River Exe to start again in Topsham and move on through Clyst St George to Woodbury, Marley, Bicton, and Littleham. Finally, the tracks passed through Exmouth eventually to come to an end in the middle of a field just south of the town.

Southern Devon was terrified. A contemporary newspaper reported that a week later 'Labourers, their wives and children, old crones and trembling old men dread to stir out after sunset, or to go out half a mile into lanes or byways on a call or message. They are under the conviction that this was the Devil's walk, and none other, and that it was wicked to trifle with such a manifest proof of the Great Enemy's immediate presence'.

Two local vicars, G.M. Musgrave of Exmouth and E.H. Ellacomb of Clyst St George, undertook a serious investigation. They took plaster casts of the prints, traced the tracks on paper, and followed the long route the mystery visitor had taken. They established that the tracks had been made between 11 pm and 4 am. What had made the tracks, they could not decide, and that remains a mystery to this day. But the people of Chudleigh Knighton know. It was the Devil.

The other phantom said to lurk near this village is a dwarf dressed all in black. He is seen most often near the bridge and he carries a shovel over his shoulder. Some say that he is trying to find his buried treasure. However, nobody has yet been brave enough to follow this odd apparition to try to find the hidden gold. After all, another story about him might be true: that is, that he could be off to dig a grave for those unwary enough to follow him.

LUTON

The mad monk of Lidwell is one of the best known phantoms of Devon. He is also one of the most disturbing. Beside the road outside Luton, west of Dawlish, stood a small wayside chapel, where a succession of holy men ministered to the spiritual needs of travellers, as well as providing welcome rest and sustenance to those caught out by approaching night or bad weather. For generations the chapel, which stood beside a well sacred to Our Lady, was a small and remote, but much respected, haven. Then it all went horribly wrong.

One evening in the 14th century a traveller was passing Luton as the light began to fail. Like so many before him, the man – he is usually said to have been a sailor – was accosted by the monk tending the chapel. Eagerly he took up the offer of a roof over his head and a hot, if modest, meal. In the course of the evening, the conversation got round to the sailor's recent voyage and the fact that he had made a tidy profit on his trading. The gold coin was in his purse and he was taking it home to his family. At this point the monk became very solicitous of the man's spiritual well being. As he had not had a chance to make confession since returning from heathen shores, the sailor followed the monk to the chapel and knelt in front of the altar. Some noise made the sailor look up. Horrified he saw the monk lunging forward, not with a Bible or rosary, but with a dagger. In the desperate fight that followed, the sailor managed to overcome the monk, knocking him unconscious. Not sure how to secure his prisoner, the sailor bundled the monk into the well and ran off in search of the forces of law and order.

It was the next day before the sailor was able to return to Lidwell chapel with a local magistrate and some armed men. As they approached, they heard the most terrible screams. The monk was found desperately trying to climb the sheer walls of the well, his fingernails torn off and his fingers made bloody by his frantic exertions. The monk was clearly out of his mind and died soon afterwards. The reason for his insanity was not difficult to find, for at the bottom of the well were the decomposing remains of his victims – over two dozen – including a mother and child. Clearly, this particular monk had been murdering travellers for their money for some time.

Ever since then, travellers passing along the Teignmouth to Exeter road have reported seeing a phantom monk hovering around the stretch of road near the ruined chapel. It is a terrifying apparition, laden with evil and madness.

The chapel lies a mile or two to the north of Luton, just off the B3192. A small car park beside a crossroads gives access to a footpath. The path goes over a stile and downhill across open land to a second stile, that gives access to a field. The small wood at the far side of the field hides the tumbledown walls where so much evil was once done.

•The South•

TORQUAY

The pleasant town of Torquay proclaims itself to be the star of the Devon Riviera. Its sweeping beaches provide safe swimming for the families that flock here in summer. The resort boomed in the early 19th century when the Napoleonic Wars stopped the gentry from travelling on the continent, and Torquay has never looked back.

The Spanish Barn at Torre Abbey in Torquay is the centre of a haunting that recalls tragic events linked to the Spanish Armada

One of the principal attractions in wet weather is Torre Abbey, a 12th century religious house that was converted into a sumptuous manor house after the dissolution of the monasteries in the 16th century. The house became the property of the Cary family, wealthy local landowners, and remained their principal seat until the 1930s, when they sold it to Torquay town council. It is now an art gallery, but the historic rooms are worth visiting in their own right.

An imposing gateway into the grounds opens onto a drive that sweeps up to the gatehouse, which still forms the main access to the ancient building. It is up this driveway that the ghostly carriage carrying Lady Cary gallops. The carriage is open, even in the wettest weather, and is pulled by a pair of grey horses. Although it is not entirely clear which of the succession of Lady Carys the ghost may be, her ballgown seems to date her to the mid-19th century. Unnervingly for those who see this impressive ghost, the horses gallop and the wheels turn in absolute silence.

A much older phantom lurks in the grounds of the abbey and has been seen pacing along nearby roads. This is the Spanish Lady. In 1588 the Spanish Armada set sail to invade England. The Spanish king, Philip II, was determined to impose Catholicism on the Protestant England of Queen Elizabeth I. The English, including those who were Catholics, preferred not to be ruled by foreigners and fought the Spanish fleet right up the Channel.

The first clash between the rival fleets was fought on 1st August off the south Devon coast. Sir Francis Drake, of course, led the English fleet into action. During the course of this early battle the Spanish galleon *Nuestra Señora del Rosario* was captured by Drake, who towed the stricken ship in triumph to Torbay. The vessel was handed over to the good folk of Torquay, while Drake and the English fleet sailed off to continue the week long fighting that saved England from Spanish rule.

The most important prisoner from the *Nuestra Señora del Rosario* was Marques Pedro de Valdés, a wealthy nobleman and highly respected soldier. He was lodged in Torre Abbey, while the 400 men who had surrendered with him were pushed into the huge abbey barn now known as the Spanish Barn. The people of Torquay took no chances with the hundreds of fit, burly and hostile Spaniards. The barn doors were locked shut and food was passed in through

The tower of St. John's church rises above the houses of central Torquay.

hatches. It was not long before disease took a hold, and many dozens of Spaniards died before they could be moved to a more suitable prison.

One of the first bodies to be passed out for burial was of a 'pageboy', but this boy turned out to be a young woman. It emerged that she was the lover of a young nobleman among the crew. The couple had expected that he would be absent from Spain for many months, perhaps years, as he played a leading role in ruling England once it had been defeated. Rather than be parted for so long, the girl had dressed as a boy and boarded the ship as her lover's page. When it was realised that the 'page' was a woman, the body was hurriedly dressed in more suitable clothes and buried in the grounds of the abbey, with a Catholic priest from among the prisoners officiating.

The ghost of this unfortunate girl has been seen walking quietly among the trees and roads near the barn ever since. She is dressed modestly in a plain dress with a small ruff, perhaps the clothes in which she was buried. There is no sign of her aristocratic lover; so perhaps he survived to return home. At any rate, the girl's ghost walks alone.

Central Torquay and the harbour are dominated by the tower of St John's church. For many years in the 19th century, this church was fortunate enough to have the distinguished musician Henry Ditton-Newman as its resident organist. He died in 1883 and startled the congregation when his ghost was seen at his own funeral. The organ he had loved so much was heard to play of its own accord several times in the following weeks. This particular ghost then faded away, but came back to St John's in the 1960s and has since continued to be seen and heard playing.

Originally a separate village, but now part of Torquay, Cockington has a reputation for being among the most haunted places in Devon. One local resident reported: 'There are more ghosts there than you can shake a stick at.' Among the phantoms seen here with regularity is the old gatekeeper. He appears at the gates to Cockington Court, stepping forwards as if to ask visitors their business. He never asks his question, but vanishes from sight in an instant. There is also a pair of phantom spaniels that gambol about near the house, and a rather sinister man dressed in 17th century costume has been seen. The churchyard has its own ghost, a woman dressed in grey who flits among the gravestones.

BUCKFASTLEIGH

During medieval times Buckfastleigh was famous for its abbey. Along with so many other religious houses, it was closed down by Henry VIII during the dissolution of the monasteries. The abbey lands were sold off, and the buildings were stripped of anything valuable and then left to fall into ruin. They were not, however, abandoned entirely. Ghostly monks were seen walking in procession through the crumbling buildings. In the mid-20th century the lands were re-acquired by the church and a new monastery was built. The ghostly monks are still seen from time to time, but the living monks are more numerous.

In the early 19th century a weaver named Dean lived in Buckfastleigh. His work was famous in the area for its quality and he worked long and hard to ensure his customers got what they asked for. In old age he died suddenly in the middle of a commission. The day after the funeral, his family were surprised to see the old man back at work, seemingly keen to finish his final job.

The modern buildings of Buckfastleigh Abbey replaced a ruined medieval structure,
although the ancient ghosts still remain.

The local vicar was called in. He bravely spoke to the phantom, but the ghost of Dean insisted that he had to finish his work before he would leave. Since the ghost could not actually work the loom, this promised to take forever. The resourceful vicar hurried back to the churchyard and scooped up a handful of earth from Dean's grave. Returning to the loom and its phantom worker, he threw the earth at the ghost. The phantom promptly vanished, to be seen no more.

A lane running west from Buckfastleigh climbs up a steep hill towards the hamlet of Wallaford. This was once home to a notoriously bad-tempered man named Squire Cabell. In life this man quarrelled with all his neighbours at one time or another and most locals preferred to give him a wide berth. Now that he is dead, it is still best to give him a wide berth. He is seen, mounted on a huge black horse, galloping down this narrow lane. Heedless of pedestrians or motorists, the squire lashes his horse to ever greater speed as he plunges down the twisting lane. When he reaches the churchyard where he is buried, the ghostly squire vanishes abruptly.

BERRY POMEROY

The massive ruins of Berry Pomeroy castle are among the premier tourist attractions in this part of south Devon. They manage to combine mighty medieval solidity with charm and a quiet atmosphere that is most endearing. They are also very haunted.

The castle was built by the family of Sir Ralph de Pomerai, a Norman knight who was given the manor of Berry by William the Conqueror in 1067. Sir Ralph had fought with William at the Battle of Hastings. The former owner of the manor, Alric, had fought on the losing side, that of King Harold, and been robbed of his estates in consequence. In the second half of the 16th century the castle was remodelled by the Seymour family, who bought Berry from the Pomeroys. An elegant Tudor mansion was built within the forbidding medieval walls. After 1700, the house and castle were abandoned and both now lie in ruins.

The gateway to Berry Pomeroy castle, which is the centre for several different hauntings.

The most famous of the many ghosts of Berry Pomeroy is the White Lady. She dates back to

*The Pomeroy girls were noted local beauties and close
sisters, but they became deadly rivals in love.*

medieval times. It is said that the Lord Pomeroy of the time had two daughters, Lady Margaret and Lady Eleanor, both equally beautiful and both infatuated with the same dashing young knight from nearby Totnes. Unfortunately, one of the girls was not as good as she was beautiful. Lady Margaret locked her sister in a dungeon, deep beneath a tower, and left her to rot, while she successfully wooed the young knight. When she was released, Lady Eleanor was too ill to survive long. She walked the ramparts a few times and then died. But she did not rest. Lady Eleanor returned to Berry Pomeroy in the white wedding dress she never wore when alive. The White Lady, as she is now known, climbs the stairs in one of the towers and walks round the ramparts. She is seen several times each year by visitors or staff and never varies her routine.

Rather more disturbing is the Blue Lady. This phantom is the ghost of a young woman dressed in a long blue dress. There can be no doubt that this ghost is determined to cause trouble. She is most often seen lurking on the edge of the tumbling walls or hovering where no floors exist. She will beckon men – it is always men – to join her. Sometimes she seems to be in trouble and asking for help in getting down from the walls. Any man who goes to help her is in danger; more than one has fallen from the walls and suffered injury.

Apparently, the Blue Lady is the sad phantom of another beautiful daughter of the Pomeroy family. This poor girl was abused by her father and incestuously gave birth to a baby boy. Unable to stand her life any longer, the distraught girl smothered the baby and hurled herself to her death from the castle walls. She would seem to have a grudge against all men and now tries to lure them into danger.

There are said to be other ghosts at Berry Pomeroy castle. A tall man in a dark suit has been seen, as have a man dressed in old-fashioned country clothes and a large black dog. None of these seen often, and other phantoms have been seen just once. It is the two women that feature in most of the sightings at Berry Pomeroy and account for the castle's reputation for being haunted.

TOTNES

The attractive little town of Totnes stands perched on a hill above the River Dart. In the 9th century, the hilltop settlement was fortified as a defence against the Viking raids that plagued England at the time. Thereafter, the place prospered and a castle, a priory and a flourishing wool town were built on the hill. And, of course, the town has acquired its ghosts.

The centre of the old town, and of the most persistent haunting, is the ancient spring of fresh water that bubbles from the ground near the top of the hill. This is known as Leech Well, taking its name from the fact that its waters were regularly prescribed by doctors – often termed 'leeches' in days gone by. The spectre that hovers around Leech Well is a woman in grey. She is seen bending over the small pool of water that forms around the spring as if stooping to drink. Sometimes she is just standing next to the spring. Occasionally she walks off along one of the narrow footpaths that link the well to the streets of the town. Local legend has it that this phantom in grey is a nun who carried water from the well for her sisters, and that she is also seen in Warland Street, where the convent had its burial ground.

In recent years, the New Age pagans, who seem to have gathered around Totnes as they have done around Glastonbury and Stonehenge, have adopted

The guildhall of Totnes was built on the site of an ancient priory and harbours a mysterious entity.

this ancient spring and spectre as their own. They hold that the grey lady is no nun, but a pre-Christian water spirit. The well, they believe, is sacred to Mother Earth and the spectre is the guardian spirit of the place. A wicker work figure of a woman has been made and put in the pool of water around the spring to be festooned with offerings and appeals for help.

A short way round the corner from the Leech Well is the Kingsbridge Inn. This pub is haunted by a woman, though she seems to be entirely different from the grey ghost of the spring. This sad spectre is of a 17th century barmaid named Mary Brown, who was seduced and made pregnant by the landlord of the inn. Being a thoroughly disreputable man, the landlord refused to marry Mary. The poor girl gave birth to her child, and then died soon afterwards. Local gossip had it that she was murdered by the landlord, but nothing was ever proved. Unlike the Blue Lady of Berry Pomeroy, this woman returns, not to take revenge on men, but apparently to warn her fellow women. She is seen only by women, usually single women. Perhaps she returns to advise them not to make the same mistake that she did when alive.

Much happier is the Victorian woman who lurks in a narrow alley that opens off Fore Street. This is a Miss Pinn, an elderly spinster who lived in this alley and acted as tutor to local girls who wished to learn the academic subjects then more usually taught to boys. She was very happy in her work and in her home. Presumably she cannot bear to leave, and so is seen wandering down the alley on frequent occasions.

In the centre of the old fortified town stands the guildhall. The present building dates largely from the 16th century, but incorporates much of the ancient priory that once stood on the site. The top of the main staircase is haunted by a shadowy figure. Most people who come across it agree it is a man, but the shifting shape is so insubstantial that it is impossible to decide the age to which he belongs.

The narrow lane outside the guildhall is Ramparts Walk, so named because it leads to the medieval ramparts that long defended the town. This lane is haunted by a tall handsome man dressed in Tudor costume. He wears a green outfit with a white ruff at his neck and a tall black hat. Whoever this dashing figure may be, he is certainly a jovial chap. He is usually said to be grinning broadly as if enjoying some private joke. It must be a good joke to have kept him amused these past four centuries.

BRIXHAM

The charming seaside town of Brixham is often overshadowed in reputation by Torquay, its northern neighbour across Torbay. It does, however, have attractions – and two ghosts – of its own.

The older and more active of the ghosts is the phantom of Squire Hilliard. In the 16th century, the local manor house, now known as The Black House, was the home of the Hilliard family. Squire Hilliard was a proud and arrogant man. He reckoned his family to be an ancient and noble one, and deeply

*Brixham harbour, where the lonely phantom of Squire Hilliard waits for
his beloved son, who never returned.*

resented the wealth that was being gained by the families of merchants and sea
rovers, such as the Drakes. When his son announced that he had fallen in love
with a local farmer's daughter from Churston, Squire Hilliard was furious. He
sent his son away and told the girl that he had died in foreign lands. The girl
was distraught but, being practical, soon accepted a proposal from a burly
farmer who stood to inherit a few acres. As bad chance would have it, young
Master Hilliard had tired of his father's instructions and was riding home on
the wedding day. He saw his beloved leaving the church with another man and
rode off in a terrible rage.

Exactly what happened next, nobody is certain. Some hours later the horse
walked home alone. A search was carried out for Master Hilliard, of course, but
no trace of him was found. Most people thought he must have killed himself,

but Squire Hilliard could not bring himself to believe he had inadvertently caused the death of his beloved son. Day after day, Squire Hilliard roamed Brixham and the surrounding area. At first, he searched in case his son had suffered an accident. Then, he looked for anyone who had seen him ride off. Always Squire Hilliard declared his boy would be back today, or maybe tomorrow. But the young man never came home. Poor Squire Hilliard died soon after, but he still wanders the streets of Brixham. He is seen most often near The Black House or around the harbour. Perhaps he hopes his son will one day come home on a ship riding the tide into a safe mooring at last.

The second phantom is that of a former vicar, the Revd Thomas Kitson. He was a much respected man and is instantly recognizable by his towering height and skinny frame. He has been seen several times riding around near the church on a white horse.

NORTH HUISH

Not the easiest place to find, the little village of North Huish is tucked away down narrow lanes among the hills south-west of Totnes. It has a gentle, calm atmosphere, and the parish church stands overlooking a green valley. It is no longer used for services, the parish of North Huish having been merged with Diptford, itself part of a grouping with nearby villages. The church still offers a place to rest, however, and the parish council has installed a bench near the tower for the use of passers-by.

Among those passers-by is

The churchyard gate at North Huish, through which the local ghost makes its way.

the phantom monk who has haunted the village since time immemorial. In the days when this was a separate parish, the ghost was often seen in the old rectory. This ancient building had been the manor house and contained a number of priest holes hidden in its thick walls. In these small cavities the Catholic family that lived here during the 16th century would hide visiting priests when inquisitive Protestant neighbours came to call. It must be assumed that the phantom monk is one such visiting priest, for no monastery ever stood at North Huish.

These days, the old rectory is a private house, and the ghost is seen most often as he walks through the gateway into the churchyard and up towards the church itself. He seems to be a peaceful, gentle phantom, who causes no trouble to anybody. Perhaps he is grateful for the new bench.

BURGH ISLAND

Lying off the Devon coast facing Bigbury on Sea is steeply sloping Burgh Island. Today, the island is linked to the mainland by a sandbar, which is uncovered at high tide. A welcoming hotel of impressive art deco design and a lifeguard station are to be found on the island. The surrounding golden beaches are cleaned daily in the summer season and are advertised as being perfect for building sandcastles, a pastime made all the more enjoyable by the kiosk selling ice creams and sweets.

But Burgh Island was not always so welcoming. In fact, time was when this was a positively dangerous place to visit. During the late 14th century the island was the base for a particularly vicious band of pirates, led by a tall swaggering man by the name of Tom Crocker.

In those turbulent years the line between piracy, patriotism, and merchant trading was not always particularly clear. Merchant ships from different kingdoms, states, and cities were often bitter rivals in trade. Some sought to gain a market for their goods by brutal intimidation of competitors rather than through quality of merchandise or low prices. Men such as Tom Crocker could earn a good living by escorting honest Devon merchants on trading voyages to

Beautiful Burgh Island is now a tourist resort, but its ghost recalls more violent days.

ensure their safety. If any foreign merchants tried to strongarm the Devon lads, a message could be sent to Tom Crocker telling him when and where the foreigners could be found.

One such ugly incident involving a band of English sailors from Sussex led to the deaths of nineteen Venetian sailors and the looting of their ship in 1374. The matter came to the notice of the King of England, Edward III, as one of the dead was the son of a nobleman. Compensation had to be paid and the guilty men were briefly imprisoned.

Crocker himself went too far in the spring of 1395. Perhaps loot to be plundered from foreigners was not plentiful enough, but, for whatever reason, Crocker and his men attacked an English ship. For the men of Devon this was too much, and in the third week of August a coordinated attack was organised by land and sea. Ships from Exeter sailed to blockade the waters off the island, while armed men lined the shore at what is now Bigbury on Sea. After a short fight, Tom Crocker was captured, dragged to the highest point on the island, and hanged.

It was not long before the ghostly figure of Tom Crocker began to be seen walking on the shores of Burgh Island. He may have been searching for buried treasure, but most believed he had been refused entry to heaven and was condemned to wander forever on the lonely, windswept beaches of his old lair. At other times, the ghostly shade of his ship was seen pulling out from Burgh Island, heading south under a full press of canvas.

These days, Burgh Island is no longer a lonely place. Windsurfers scud across the waters and holidaymakers throng the sands. It seems that the phantom pirate from so many years ago is now seen only in August, around the anniversary of his death. His ghost ship has not been seen for years. Perhaps the old sea rover does not appreciate the modern invasion of his formerly remote hideaway.

CORNWOOD

The village of Cornwood lies on the southern edge of Dartmoor, and the roads that lead here go nowhere in particular, merely petering out as they reach the edge of the high moor.

This rather remote village was once home to the Raleigh family. Unlike many of the Devon families who made their fortunes on the high seas during the Tudor and Stuart years, the Raleighs were an established part of the local gentry, owning land and manors. The most famous member of the family to have lived at Cornwood was Sir Walter Raleigh. He began his colourful career as a soldier, joining the Protestant Huguenots in the religious wars of France in the 1560s and then joining the English army fighting the Earl of Desmond in Ireland in 1580.

In 1581 Raleigh was chosen to carry the dispatches proclaiming victory in

Ireland to Elizabeth I. The dashing young man at once won the approval and favour of the queen. According to popular legend, he had bought an expensive outfit for his first appearance at court. When walking with her courtiers, the queen was faced by a muddy puddle; she hesitated, and the courtiers likewise held back. But Raleigh whisked off his costly cloak and laid it over the mud for the queen to step across. Whether there is any truth in the story is uncertain, but Raleigh was certainly popular with the great and glorious Elizabeth.

Over the following 20 years, Raleigh used his contacts at court to secure lucrative business contracts and to acquire spreading acres. He sailed on voyages of exploration to North and South America, served in Parliament, fought the Spanish, and wrote an impressive historical work. He introduced potatoes from the Americas to Britain, planting them extensively on his estates. In 1603, Elizabeth died, and Raleigh's influence at court, already diminshed, died with her. He was arrested on the orders of the new king, James I, and thrown into the Tower of London on trumped up charges of treason. In 1618, King James needed to win the favour of Spain, so he ordered the execution of Raleigh whose exploits on the Spanish Main had not been forgotten.

Raleigh's widow, Elizabeth Throgmorton, abandoned London and the court, retiring to Raleigh's estates. According to local legend, she went to Cornwood together with Raleigh's fortune. She jealously guarded the revenues from the family estates and kept a careful watch over the Raleigh wealth. After she died, the Raleigh heirs found that the estates were well-run and the accounts in perfect order. But of Lady Elizabeth's accumulated gold there was no sign. A small chest with a few coins was found, but no trace of the vast store of wealth that the accounts indicated must exist could be turned up.

Soon after her death, the phantom of the dead Lady Elizabeth began to walk the lanes and fields around Cornwood. She is now known as the Dark Lady, for she wears a long dress of heavy dark silk, which rustles as she walks. Whether the ghost is seeking to lead people to her lost treasure, or is guarding it from intruders, is not known; nobody who has seen her has stayed around long enough to find out. The Dark Lady of Cornwood seems fated to wander forever around this beautiful stone village beneath the looming mass of Dartmoor.

PLYMOUTH

Plymouth used to be one of the best preserved historic cities in England. A writer in the late 19th century declared, 'The sea front of Plymouth is the most interesting spot within the British Empire, if not the most beautiful also.' Others had similar views, and the number of ancient buildings there was great. Then Hitler's Luftwaffe came to rain down bombs on the mighty naval docks, and flattened most of the city centre as well.

Many ghosts lost their old haunts in the devastating air raids, but one which did not is the phantom of Plymouth's most famous inhabitant. Sir Francis Drake was born near Tavistock. After making his fortune, he lived at Buckland Abbey, but for most of his life his home was in Plymouth. In 1567 he commanded the tiny 50 ton ship *Judith* as part of a trading fleet sailing to the Gulf of Mexico. The Spanish governor at one port agreed that the English ships could enter port; the Spaniards then treacherously opened fire and seized most of the English ships and their goods. Drake's ship was one of the few to escape. He never forgave the Spanish nor passed up an opportunity to attack and plunder the Spanish Empire.

In 1588 England was at war with Spain, and the mighty Spanish Armada set sail to land an invasion army in England. Drake was appointed second in command of the English fleet and ordered as many ships as possible to meet in Plymouth to await the arrival of the Spanish. The commander of the fleet was Lord Howard. Custom of the time dictated that a nobleman had to lead any national force, but Drake was undoubtedly the man the seamen looked to for inspiration and instruction.

On 29th July, a small ship raced into Plymouth Sound. An officer was rowed ashore and he at once asked for Drake. He was directed towards the grassy open space known as Plymouth Hoe, where Drake and his fellow captains were playing a game of bowls. Breathless from a fast run up the hill, the officer burst in on the game to declare that the Spanish Armada had been sighted to the west of Lizard Point.

Many of the captains gathered their belongings and fussed about, seeking

61

*A Victorian painting shows Drake's ship attacking the
Spanish galleon* Nuestra Senova.

instructions or issuing contradictory orders. Drake, realising that morale and steady thinking would be paramount in the coming battle, told the captains to calm down. 'There is time to finish our game, and beat the Spanish too,' he declared. No doubt his coolness was helped by the fact that it was 5 pm and he knew that the tide would not allow any ships to leave Plymouth until 9 pm.

It is fitting that the phantom of Sir Francis Drake should be seen on the Hoe. Not only was this the scene of the famous bowls match, but it was here that he and generations of other Plymouth seamen have come to watch for the return of ships to port. Drake is seen standing quietly on the Hoe, gazing out to sea. No doubt his mind is on the far, rolling ocean, where he spent so much of his life.

A very different phantom of Sir Francis is to be encountered on the rocky promontory to the west, known as Devil's Point. The Spanish fervently believed that Drake had made a pact with the Devil. How else, they reasoned, could a Protestant heretic have such luck with the weather and with his many exploits? The story got to England, and rumours of the origin of the famous Drake's luck soon spread.

It was said that in the weeks before the Armada came, Drake would climb up to Devil's Point to discuss the situation with his evil patron. One night, so the story goes, Drake and a group of magicians gathered on Devil's Point to indulge in infernal incantations and spells. The result was the dreadful storm which scattered the Spanish Armada in the North Sea and ensured that so few of the ships would survive to return to Spain. And on wild and stormy nights, Drake's phantom is seen there still waving his arms and brewing up a tempest with the Devil's help.

ASHLEIGH BARTON

A few miles north of Plymouth stands Ashleigh Barton. This tiny settlement, comprising little more than a farm and a couple of cottages, seems on the brink of being engulfed by the housing estates and factories of Plymouth that lie just over the hill to the south.

The female ghost who lurks beside the road junction here is not a ghost that anyone would want to encounter. Nobody seems to know who she is or what her connection is to this place. But everyone is agreed that she is to be shunned, for it is said that the only reason this spectre appears is to announce the approaching death of a member of the family of whoever sees her.

It is, perhaps, best that this road junction should remain quiet and largely ignored. If too many people were to pass this way, there is no telling what the White Lady of Ashleigh Barton might get up to.

BUCKLAND ABBEY

The peaceful and beautiful abbey at Buckland has had a chequered history, which is reflected in its diverse and numerous collection of phantoms.

The abbey, a Cistercian monastery, was built in 1278 on land in a secluded wooded valley granted by Amicia, Countess of Devon. It was the last Cistercian abbey to be founded in England and, at first, it housed only twelve monks. The ghosts of these medieval monks are the oldest to be seen at Buckland. Usually only a lone monk is seen, but sometimes a small procession winds its way through long-vanished corridors or rooms.

Over the years the abbey grew in size until, by 1539, it was an impressive and wealthy establishment. In that year the abbey was seized by the Crown as part of the dissolution of the monasteries. The buildings and lands were sold to the Grenville family, who made few changes and in 1581 sold Buckland Abbey to Sir Francis Drake. Drake, newly wealthy as a result of his voyage around the world and his plundering of

Sir Francis Drake, whose drum remains at his old home in Buckland Abbey, to be sounded should England need to summon his spirit to repel foreign invaders.

Spanish galleons, at once set about converting the old buildings into a sumptuous country mansion. The nave of the church was split by the insertion of two floors, and each storey was divided into rooms. Other buildings were pulled down or converted, and new buildings were put up.

According to local gossip, Drake accomplished the renovations in just three days and nights, without the aid of workmen. He achieved this, it was whispered, with the help of the Devil, with whom he was in league. It was because of this supposed pact with the Evil One, that Drake has been doomed to periodically drive a coach of startling appearance out of Buckland Abbey and across high, windswept Dartmoor to Tavistock. The coach, it is said, is pure black and pulled by four jet black horses, which Drake whips into a wild-eyed gallop. Behind the coach comes a pack of gigantic black hounds, baying and slavering as if on the trail of a prey.

Kept on a table in the great hall of Buckland Abbey is the house's most famous possession: Drake's drum. It is known that Drake had a great attachment to this instrument. It was the drum used on board his ship during his voyage around the world to rouse the crew to action stations or dismiss them for meals. The same drum was with Drake when he died of dysentery during yet another raid on the Spanish Empire – this time to the West Indies – in 1596. His men brought the drum back to Devon and gave it to Drake's younger brother and heir, Thomas. Thomas installed it in the great hall, and, except for restoration in 1910, it has never left.

It is said that as he lay dying, Drake made a promise. He declared that, if ever the Spanish sent another Armada to invade England, as they had done just eight years earlier, then his men should play a loud tattoo on his drum. Then, said Drake, he would come back from the dead with guns firing to lead the English fleet against the foreign enemy once again.

The Spanish never did send another invasion fleet, but that does not mean that the drum has been silent. Although no human hands have dared to play the instrument since Drake's death, the drum has sounded of its own accord. It throbbed loudly in August 1914 as war was being declared against Germany, and again in September 1940 when Hitler's armies stood at Calais poised to invade England. It has not been heard to beat since.

GUNNISLAKE

It was at Gunnislake that for centuries the River Tamar, which forms the boundary between Devon and Cornwall, could first be bridged. There is now a modern toll bridge miles downstream near Plymouth, but the old bridge over the Tamar at Gunnislake remains busy with through traffic between the two counties.

It is also the place where the terrifying phantom of Dando crosses the river. For years Dando was one of the most disliked men in the area. He was a monk at the priory of St German's in Cornwall during the 13th century, but Dando was no ordinary monk. He had joined the Church because his father had made a sacred vow that his youngest son would be dedicated to God and, as the youngest son, Dando was duly sent to the cloisters when still a boy.

As he grew older, however, Dando found he had no real liking for the bookish and celibate life of the monastery. He wrote to his family asking for money, which, he promised, would be handed over to the deserving poor of St German's. In truth, Dando invested the money in a fine black stallion and a suit of elegant clothes. He would take off his monk's robes, don his secular clothes, mount his horse and ride out of Cornwall over the bridge at Gunnislake to Devon. There he would spend his family's gold on drink, gambling, and loose women. As the years passed, Dando became increasingly debauched. He would get drunk, start fights, seduce maidens, and generally behave in the worst way possible. He used his gold to buy off those he injured, and hired toughs to beat up those who did not take his gold.

But retribution was catching up with Dando. One day he was out hunting with some cronies along the banks of the Tamar when another hunter appeared, dressed all in black and leading a pack of black hounds. He pulled up alongside Dando and leaned down to offer a large flask filled with ale; and Dando who was thirsty, drank deeply.

'Had much luck with your hunting?' Dando asked the man in black, pointing to his own stag to show he had made a kill.

'Not until now' declared the stranger. He at once threw off his cloak to

The bridge over the Tamar at Gunnislake, the scene of a terrifying encounter with the Devil which led to a famous haunting.

reveal that he was none other than the Devil. In a sudden fright, Dando put his spurs to his horse and rode at breakneck speed for the bridge at Gunnislake. If only he could cross the river and make it to the holy ground of St German's, he would be safe. He never made it. The Devil caught up with Dando beside the bridge, knocked him from his horse, and dragged him into the swirling waters of the Tamar.

It was not long before Dando came back from the hell to which he had condemned himself. This time he led the pack of great black hounds as they raced along the banks of the Tamar. But he did not hunt stags or deer, not any more, now Dando was after the souls of the damned to take back to his master, the Devil. Those who hear a pack of hounds baying after their quarry along the Tamar near Gunnislake usually do not stay around to see if it is Dando. They never know if they might be the quarry.

DARTMOOR

T he wild bleak beauty of Dartmoor has long had a romantic appeal for many. The heather moorland, grassy hills, and deep gorges with their rocky rivers

The bleak heights of Crockern Tor, which are haunted by a skeletal phantom.

are home to thousands of sheep as well as to the Dartmoor ponies, whose surefootedness and rugged constitution are world famous. The high moorland covers around 150 square miles, and the fringes of the moor extend much further. The whole area is covered by the Dartmoor National Park regulations, while smaller areas have been set aside as nature reserves, Sites of Special Scientific Interest, and listed archaeological sites.

Dartmoor is not just wild and beautiful; it is special too, and it has its ghosts. Some of them are rather enigmatic. Crockern Tor, for instance, takes its name from the ghostly man who haunts its rocky summit. This is Crockern, who rides around on a skeleton horse. Who Crockern was and why he haunts this windy spot, nobody seems to know.

Equally obscure in origin or purpose is the phantom of Clasiwell. Clasiwell is a spring of freshwater that forms a pool near Burra Tor. The haunting manifests itself as a disembodied voice, which seems to boom out from the middle of the waters. It shouts predictions at passers by, though these predictions are not always easy to interpret. It is said that one recipient of the dubious advice of the Clasiwell phantom was Piers Gaveston, who passed this way in 1311. Gaveston, the favourite of Edward II, was in disgrace at the time. His sharp tongue and habit of helping himself from the royal finances had angered the kingdom's leading nobles, who had compelled him to retire from court to his lands in Devon. When passing Clasiwell, Gaveston heard the voice shouting, 'Your humbled head will soon be high.' Taking this to mean he would be restored to favour, Gaveston rode back to court. The furious nobles gave him no second chance, but murdered him and hoisted his head high on a spike above the gates of Warwick.

There are times that are better than others for finding some of the ghosts of Dartmoor. Nights of the full moon are the time when the ghostly warriors of Hunter's Tor put in an appearance. These have the look of ancient ghosts indeed, for they carry weapons made of bronze and wear bronze armour. This would seem to date them to the Bronze Age, a period some 4,000 years ago. This is not impossible. Dartmoor was then an area with a relatively high population. The climate during this period favoured the uplands, while the simple ploughs of the time were better suited to the thin upland soil than the rich, but heavy, soil of the lowlands.

Also seen when the full moon shines on the moor are the phantoms of Bowerman's Nose. The tall pillar of natural rock which stands up from the moor at this point is, according to legend, all that remains of a hunter who

The ancient warriors of Hunter's Tor

interrupted the proceedings of a witches' coven and was turned to stone for his impudence. It is not his ghost, however, but those of the witches that return on moonlit nights to dance on the heather.

Another place that is best avoided is Wistman's Wood, which lies north of Two Bridges. It is in this area that the Devil emerges from Hell to hunt for the souls of the damned. He appears in the guise of an expensively dressed gentleman mounted on a black stallion and accompanied by a pack of black hounds. An old legend tells of a shepherd who had been fortifying himself against the cold with mugs of cider when he saw the Devil returning from his hunt. Presumably the cider gave the man courage, for he asked the Devil if he had enjoyed good sport. The Devil laughed and said he had, tossing a body to the ground. The shepherd was horrified to see it was the body of his own son.

Rather better documented is the ghost of Childe's Tomb, a heap of stones topped by a stone cross that stands on the moor a mile from the nearest road at Whiteworks. Back in the 1340s, a rich merchant from Plymstock, named Childe, was riding home across the moor when he was suddenly caught in a freezing blizzard. This is a particularly bleak spot and no shelter at all offered itself. In desperation, Childe killed and disembowelled his horse, and then climbed inside the carcass for warmth. He survived for some time, but eventually felt death over coming him. Childe pulled a scrap of paper from his

The death of Tom Pearse's grey mare.

pocket and wrote on it: 'The first that brings me to my grave, my lands at Plymstock he shall have.'

There then followed a rather unseemly scramble to get poor Childe decently buried. The race was won by the monks of Tavistock, who thus gained Childe's lands. Ever since, a procession of hooded monks has been seen in the winter months walking from Childe's Tomb in the direction of Tavistock.

Another ghostly funeral procession can be seen making its way along the ancient Lych Way, now a footpath. Dartmoor falls within the parish of Lydford, so the baptisms, weddings, and funerals of Dartmoor's scattered inhabitants took place in the church in that village. The Lych Way ran down from the high moor towards Lydford. On its higher stretches over the moor, the footpath is the haunt of a group of seven men, six of whom carry a coffin while the seventh leads the way with head bowed. Who these people are no one now remembers, but some strong emotion must have gripped them in their lifetimes for their spirits to keep reburying the person in the coffin. Are they desolate at losing him or do they want to make sure he is safely buried and out of the way?

By far the most famous of the Dartmoor ghosts is the white mare which gallops over the hills near the village of Widecombe in the Moor. Widecombe is a typical English village, tucked away in a fertile valley amid the bleak moorland. In past centuries it was the venue for a famous fair that attracted farmers and others from all across the moor. In time, one particular event associated with the fair led to the haunting and became celebrated in a local folksong. There are several different versions of the song, each of which commemorates a different local character and his foibles. The best known version was collected in the late 19th century by the Revd S. Baring-Gould of Lewtrenchard.

This version of the song runs:

Tom Pearse, Tom Pearse, lend me your grey mare,
Ri-fol-diddle-ol, diddle-I-do
That I may ride out to Widecombe Fair
Wi' Bill Brewer, Jan Stewer, Peter Gurney, Peter Davy, Dan'l Whiddon,
Harry Hawk, Old Uncle Tom Cobley and all.

When shall I have my old mare home again?
Ri-fol-diddle-ol, diddle-I-do
A Friday night or a Saturday morn
With Bill Brewer etc.

Needless to say, nothing is seen of Bill Brewer and his cronies or of Tom Pearce's mare until tom finds her 'upon a hill . . . making her will. The poor mare dies but,

When the wind whistles cold on the moor of a night
Ri-fol-diddle-ol, diddle-I-do
Tom Pearse's old mare doth appear gashly white
With Bill Brewer etc.

And all the night long be heard skirling and groans
Ri-fol-diddle-ol, diddle-I-do
From Tom Pearse's old mare in her rattling bones.
With Bill Brewer etc.

The stretch of road near Postbridge where many unexplained road accidents have taken place.

Of the various characters, the only one to survive in all known versions is Old Uncle Tom Cobley. This gentleman farmer lived at Buttsford Farm in the parish of Colebrooke and died in 1844. His gravestone still stands in the churchyard. He was known for his hospitality and warm humour; so no doubt he may have enjoyed being linked to the phantom white mare.

While any of these moorland spectres can be rather startling, none of them is dangerous. But the ghost of Postbridge has claimed its victims, if local stories are to be believed. The phantom takes the peculiar form of a pair of disembodied hairy hands. These are said to grab the steering wheel of passing cars, wrenching sideways to send the vehicle skidding off the road. The stories started circulating in 1921, after a popular local doctor was killed here in a motor accident. His children, who survived the crash, reported that just before the fatal crash the doctor had exclaimed that something was pulling the wheel. Soon afterwards a coach crashed at the same spot, followed by a motorcyclist before the end of the year. Accidents have continued to happen on this straight stretch of road ever since, and no real reason has been found for them – other than the hairy hands, of course.

TAVISTOCK

The town of Tavistock takes its name from the River Tavy, which flows through the town. This river is said to be the fastest flowing river in England and, during the medieval period, its soft waters were used for the washing and fulling of the woollen cloth on which the town's prosperity rested.

Tavistock has several phantoms to disturb its apparent calm. The oldest are unlikely to be encountered by the casual visitor. They are seen not in Russell Square, which dominates the town centre, but beneath it. The cellars of several properties around the square extend below the pavements and roadway. These cellars date back centuries and originally belonged to the grand Benedictine abbey which was founded here in 974 and which, until its closure in the 16th century, owned the entire town. The phantoms that have been seen in the cellars are, as perhaps might be expected, monks. There are two of them, walking quickly with arms folded.

One of the more peculiar remnants of the old monastery of Tavistock is the belief that at midnight on Midsummer's Eve the apparitions of all those citizens of the town who will die in the coming year form a procession into the church. The procession can be seen only by those who sit in the church porch and peek into the church.

On Midsummer's Eve 1795, a young man by the name of Lugger declared that he was going to sit in the porch to see who he would see. The young man had been drinking and no amount of pleading from his friends would stop him. A few minutes after midnight, young Lugger came running back to his friends, wide eyed and obviously deeply disturbed. Who had he seen, his friends asked. Lugger gasped and croaked out a single word: 'Myself.' He was dead within a week.

The best known ghost of Tavistock, however, is that of Judge Glanville, who haunts the grounds of Kilworthy House. In life John Glanville was a wealthy merchant of Tavistock. He had Kilworthy House built as a home to reflect his wealth and status and Glanville served as a Justice of the Peace for the area. As a local man, he was expected to know local circumstances, to know who could

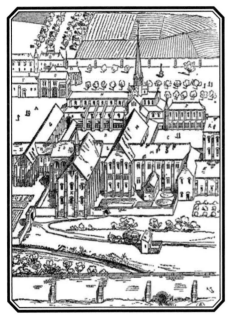

A reconstruction of the wealthy and powerful Benedictine abbey which dominated the centre of Tavistock throughout the medieval period.

or could not be trusted, and how best to enforce the king's peace.

Glanville had a daughter named Elizabeth, who fell in love with a local sailor by the name of George. The worthy merchant saw fit to overrule his daughter's feelings and insisted that she marry a rich goldsmith from Plymouth named Page. Page was fairly old and not in the best of health; so perhaps young Elizabeth reasoned she would not have to put up with matters for too long. However, seeing his sweetheart with Page for even a few months proved to be too much for the distressed George, who soon turned up in Plymouth.

Over the following weeks, the young lovers reignited their passions and decided that they could not wait for the elderly Page to pass away naturally. They would help him on his way. One night Elizabeth's maid, who seems to have been totally devoted to her, let George into the house after dark. The young man crept upstairs and strangled the old goldsmith before slipping out the way he had come.

Unfortunately for the lovers, a neighbour had seen George go into the house with more secrecy than seemed decent. When it was announced the old man had died of a seizure, the neighbour was suspicious and went to the authorities. The evidence of strangulation was quite clear, and the guilty trio were brought to trial. As fate would have it, the judge sitting on the bench that day was none other than Judge Glanville. The jury found all three guilty of murder, and so

Judge Glanville pronounced the death sentence on his own daughter.

The ghosts of both the judge and his daughter have been seen around Kilworthy House, which is now a school. The judge is seen most often walking morosely around the grounds. The daughter is usually seen inside the house, mostly near the main staircase. She quite often wears a cloak with a hood, as if she is about to slip out of the house in bad weather. Sometimes the door to the courtyard will open and slam shut, and this is usually blamed on the phantom girl.

Lydford

The straggling village of Lydford runs for hundreds of yards along the high street. Today, it is a quiet and peaceful little place, but in the Middle Ages it was a flourishing centre of the tin mining industry and a bustling town.

The money generated by tin mining brought much official activity here. There was a royal mint in the town, and the smelting of lead and silver was carried out on an almost industrial scale. There was also a royal court which handed down severe sentences for those who transgressed the stannary laws, which imposed hefty taxes on the mining and smelting industries. A local ditty runs:

I oft have heard of Lydford Law

How in the morn they hang and draw

And sit in judgement after.

At least two of the three ghosts in this village owe their sad existence to the notorious Lydford Law.

Dominating the centre of the village is the massive bulk of Lydford castle. This square granite tower set on a high mound of earth was always more of a prison than a castle. Its walls plunge as deep below the ground as they stand above and hide dank dark dungeons, where all manner of terrible deeds may have been done. Within these grim walls, the first ghost is to be found. It is reported to be a dark, opaque cloud, which is shaped something like a man, but which sometimes seems more like a pig. Whatever this is, it exudes a feeling of

Lydford Castle Inn has a phantom who lurks upstairs in Room 6.

deep evil and malevolence, and few who have seen it care to stay around to look too closely.

Beside the castle stands the altogether more welcoming Lydford Castle Inn. In the days when the castle was a prison, this was the home of the gaoler. Parts of the building date back to the rebuilding of Lydford after the Viking raid of 997, in which the entire town was destroyed, but most of the present structure is about 500 years old. It is the ghost of one of the gaolers who lurks in this building. He is seen most often upstairs, in and around room 6. This phantom is reported to be a broad muscular man dressed in workman-like clothes, who stomps noisily out of room 6 and along the corridor, giving the impression of setting out to work with grim determination. The pub has been the scene of other odd phenomena, such as a shifting white mist, which forms, drifts about, and vanishes, and to unaccountable spots and blurs that show up on photographs taken inside the building.

Many years ago a stranger came to Lydford on business. It was a foggy evening when he arrived, and he was grateful to find the usual warm welcome at the inn. While tucking into a hearty meal, the man happened to remark to his host that he had ridden down from Brent Tor. The landlord was incredulous, for the bridge over the Lydford Gorge had been washed away in a flood only the previous week and had not yet been repaired. The stranger turned white, for he recalled how, in a thick patch of mist, his horse had made a sudden leap. Retracing his route the next morning, the man saw the deep marks left by the hooves of his horse as it had jumped across the deep gorge. As can be seen by those who visit the gorge, this was a mighty leap for any horse.

The spectacular gorge is the reason for most people's visit to Lydford these days. It is a narrow ravine, down which flows the River Lyd towards the ford which gives the village its name. At the head of the gorge are the White Lady Falls. These take their name not from a ghost but from the fact that when the river is in spate they take on the shape of a bride in a flowing dress.

The ghost of the gorge, the Red Lady, is seen further downstream. Wearing a red shawl around her shoulders and pulled up over her head, she sits beside the fast-flowing stream, staring morosely into the swirling waters. No story is attached to this phantom and nobody knows who she is, but it is generally reckoned best to avoid her.

LEWTRENCHARD

The history of the village of Lewtrenchard is closely connected to that of the Gould family. And the Goulds provide the ghosts of the village as well as its history.

The oldest of the three ghosts is Susannah Gould, who died in 1729. Although a member of the family by marriage, not birth, Susannah loved the land around Lewtrenchard with all the fervour of a Gould. After her death she was seen walking beside the stream that runs through the village, and the pale woman in a flowing dress has been seen walking quietly through the lower fields as recently as 2001.

Altogether more troublesome, both alive and dead, was Lady Margaret

The parish church of Lewtrenchard.

Gould, who died in 1795. Some indication of her character may be gained from the fact that she was known far and wide as the 'Old Madam'. No doubt, she would have maintained that she needed to be able to put the fear of God into certain people. Her son was a notorious spendthrift. Although he had no malice in him, he would have worked his way through the Gould family fortune in no time if his mother had not kept him on a tight rein. The ghost of the redoubtable Old Madam was first felt at the instant of her death. At the moment she breathed her last, every window and door in the manor house flew open of its own accord. Less than an hour later, a local farmer coming to pay his respects to his bereaved landlord was startled to see the figure of the deceased striding up the drive towards him. The Old Madam paid the man no attention, but marched straight past him towards the church. Since then, she has been seen on numerous occasions, very often when some damage is done to the house she loved so much. The mere breaking of a window can be enough to cause the Old Madam to walk.

The most gentle of these phantoms is that of the Revd Sabine Baring-Gould. Rather a retiring man, Sabine Baring was enjoying a quiet living in East Anglia when his uncle died and bequeathed him the Gould estates. He managed to engineer a transfer to take up the living at Lewtrenchard, so that he enjoyed the status of both squire and vicar in this village. Once in Devon, the new vicar undertook the restoration of the parish church, which had not had much money spent on it since the 1520s. Young Sabine collected church furniture from far and wide, bringing a brass chandelier from Malines in Belgium and the altar painting from Switzerland. The lectern came from France, the triptych from Flanders, and the east window from Germany. The magnificent rood screen is one of the few local pieces to be included in Sabine's remodelled church.

There can be no doubt of the vicar's love for his church. So it comes as no surprise to learn that this gentle man and eminent folklorist continues to roam the church and its grounds. He is not seen often, but when he does appear he seems to be simply standing and enjoying his surroundings. Since he largely created them, he has a right to do so.

CHAGFORD

The summer of 1642 was a difficult one for England – and for Chagford in particular. King Charles I was embroiled in bitter and protracted disputes with Parliament; the Church of England was split by doctrinal differences; and fights broke out with alarming ease.

In July, Sir John Hotham, Governor of Hull, slammed the city gates in the face of the king. Without instructions from Parliament to allow him in, Hotham refused the King access to the fortress city, with its vast stores of military equipment. Charles saw this as a declaration of open rebellion by the forces of Parliament. On 22nd August he raised the royal standard in Nottingham and sent out orders to his loyal supporters throughout the country.

One of those who received the king's summons was the young poet Sydney Godolphin. As the head of the powerful Godolphin family, Sydney was one of the most influential men in Cornwall. He raised a force of armed men and set about attacking the supporters of Parliament. Godolphin and his men ranged widely through Cornwall, Devon, and Somerset. They demanded that tax be paid in advance, taking it at swordpoint from those who tried to refuse. They seized horses, weapons, and transport from known supporters of Parliament, impounding them for the king's use. Throughout these exploits, Godolphin managed to restrain his men from outright looting, and maintained a dashing and colourful reputation. Even his opponents had to admit that he behaved well.

Chagford at that time was a prosperous small town and a centre of the mining industry. It was inevitable that Godolphin and his men would descend on Chagford sooner or later, and the local Parliamentarians were ready for him. As the Cavaliers rode into the market place, they were met by a hail of shots from the waiting Roundheads. Godolphin was wounded but managed to get to the strongly-built stone porch of the Three Crowns Hotel. With drawn sword he held off the vengeful Roundheads, but after a spirited fight was cut down and died on the flagstones.

It is this romantic figure that haunts the Three Crowns. As might be expected, he is seen most often in the porch or near the front door, though his tall stately figure may also appear purposefully striding around in almost any part of the building.

GIDLEIGH

The village of Gidleigh stands on a steep hill where Blackawton Brook tumbles down into the River Teign. The ruins of an old castle crown the hill above the village, and it seems likely that some long forgotten incident in the castle's history has led to the more famous of the hauntings in this village.

Below the village, the road that runs up to the castle crosses the brook by way of a narrow stone bridge, which was built at about the same time as the castle. It is on this bridge that the air can turn suddenly chill and silent. The sounds of swords clashing, men cursing, and clanking armour then fill the air

The stone bridge at Gidleigh, the home of a pair of violently combative phantoms.

for a few seconds, before fading away. The temperature returns to normal as suddenly as it fell. One witness, who experienced this haunting in 1999, reported that he saw a pair of knights in armour fighting each other. The spectres were in view for only a second, and then vanished.

Gidleigh would seem not to have been an easy place for women to live in days gone by. On the high moor, just outside the village, stands the prehistoric stone circle of Scorhill. Around 60 boulders were set upright in a circle about 80 feet across by the people who lived here 4,000 years ago. Much later this circle became the focus for a ritual which unfaithful wives or promiscuous young women were forced to perform. The unfortunate women first had to bathe naked in the Cranmere pool near Okehampton. Then, clad only in a shirt, they had to walk to the River Teign below Gidleigh to bathe again. They were then taken to the Scorhill circle, where they had to kneel in front of the tallest stone and beg forgiveness for their sins. If nothing happened, the woman was deemed to be forgiven for her actions, and had to be taken back by her husband. Sometimes, however, the stone would topple forward and crush the woman to death. The dozen or so fallen stones, it is said, bear witness to the fact that this punishment has occurred on occasion.

It is, perhaps, one of the unfortunate women who perished under the stones who now returns in spectral form as the Grey Lady of Gidleigh. She walks, with her head bowed, from the River Teign, up the banks of Blackawton Brook. One story has it that she was a faithless wife who drowned herself in the river rather than endure the very public humiliation involved in the Scorhill ritual.

There used to be another phantom lurking near Gidleigh, and a most horrible one it was. There lived on the high moor a giant who ate only sheep, grabbed by his violent hands from the flocks of the good people of the area. Folk knew he was about when a fire was seen flickering up on the moor and the roasted bones of a sheep were found scattered around next morning. This giant has not been seen for many years, and, some may suspect, he was in reality just a human poacher at work. Whatever the truth, the legend persists.

WONSON

The Northmoor Arms at Wonson is a fine and ancient building. Quite how old it actually is remains unclear. Certainly the inn is 400 years old, and parts of it may date back another two centuries or more. Whatever its age, it was the scene of a famous game of cards in the 1660s. The stern rule of the puritan Parliamentarians, which followed the defeat of the king in the civil wars, had borne down harshly on areas such as Devon where Royalist support had been strong. Armed soldiers were billeted with hapless households, both to ensure good behaviour and to relieve the government of the cost of feeding the men. Among the more unpopular rules of the new regime was the prohibition of most leisure pursuits. The Puritans in government preferred to worship God rather than go to the theatre, dance, or play cards, and they saw no reason why anyone else should indulge in such frivolous pursuits either. Even Christmas feasts were banned.

So, when King Charles II came to the throne in the 1660s, he courted

The pub at Wonson which was once the scene of a game of cards that led to a haunting.

popularity by lifting the prohibitions on having a good time, and soon became known as the Merry Monarch. And few places were merrier than Wonson. The owner of the Northmoor Arms was one of those determined to enjoy his new freedoms to the full. Feasts, dances, and entertainments of every kind were staged here.

Unfortunately, one night the good times went too far. The landlord found that he had gambled his fortune away; even the deeds to Northmoor Arms had passed across the gaming table. The impoverished man packed up a few personal belongings and left, never to be seen in Wonson again.

At least, he was never seen in the village alive. Some years later, however, presumably after he had died in some distant part of the country, the former owner reappeared at the inn. He did not come alone, but with three companions, and the four ghosts are seen from time to time to this day. The downstairs bar is their favourite haunt. Usually, they are to be observed sitting together in a corner of the room, quietly minding their own business. Sometimes, though, they play cards. Perhaps the ghosts replay for all eternity that fateful game of so long ago.

TETCOTT

Perhaps the kindest thing that could be said about the Arscott family of Tetcott is that a great many of them were a bit odd. Their eccentricities made a lasting impression on the village and more than one ghost remains to bear witness to their story.

One member of the family seems to have positively aimed to be remembered as the achetypal wicked squire. His fights, seductions, gambling, and vicious temper were legendary. Although his body is buried in Tetcott churchyard, local legend has it that his soul was forbidden to follow it into sacred ground and was imprisoned in an oak tree by the churchyard gates. His ghost is seen here, bewailing his fate.

A dwarf, known only as Black Jack, lived for many years in Tetcott as the chief entertainer to the Arscotts. He hired players and musicians to come to the village, and could put on a few stunts of his own. He could, for instance, tie mice by the legs and lower them down his throat, pulling them back alive from his stomach. As he grew older, Black Jack sometimes fell into trance-like fits. After one he declared that he had met the Devil and been taken down to Hell. When asked what it was like, he replied, 'Just like here in winter, with the Arscotts nearest the fire.'

The most colourful of the Arscott ghosts is John Arscott, the last of his line. He was a dedicated huntsman who rode out with his pack of hounds whenever he had the chance. A few days after his death, the pack of hounds suddenly grew very restless and, in what seemed to be a collective madness, they broke out of their kennels and raced off over the fields – perhaps to join a master only they could see? Since then, the phantom of John Arscott has been seen riding his black stallion across the fields, as recalled in a local ditty:

When the full moon is shining as clear as day
John Arscott still hunteth the country, they say,
You may see him on Blackbird, and hear in full cry
The pack from Pencarrow to Dazzard go by.

The Arscott family, which had once so dominated this area of Devon, died out in 1788, and the estates then passed to the Molesworth family. Being landed gentry in Ireland, the Molesworths had little time for Tetcott. They pulled down the manor house, selling the salvage for cash, and disposed of the estates.

HATHERLEIGH

The little village of Hatherleigh, now returned to its rural quiet since the building of a bypass for the A386, has an unusual collection of phantoms.

The George Hotel has two diverse apparitions. The first is a monk or clergyman who walks the ground floor. This ghost is seen with such regularity that the main bar has been named the 'Mad Monk's Bar' in his honour. He is, however, a gentle soul who causes no real problems to anyone. It is merely the sudden surprise of encountering him that can upset the visitor. The other ghost is seen upstairs; so her path does not cross that of the monk. This is probably just as well. Not only is this ghost young, female, and attractive – enough to worry many a devout monk – she is also stark naked. This ghost is seen much less often than the monk, which may be a disappointment to some customers.

When a new landlady, Janice, moved in to the George in 1999, one of the phantoms decided to welcome her to the inn. One morning Janice decided to move around some of the pictures in the restaurant. Within a few hours the pictures had leapt from the wall and tumbled face down on the ground, although neither the hooks on the walls nor the wires on the pictures were broken. Janice is sure that the ghost is a gentle soul who was just letting her know that he was in the George first.

Just north of the village the land climbs steeply to Beaford Moor. This windswept, bleak patch of land is crossed by the A386 on its way to Okehampton. It is here that the Black Dog of Beaford runs through the mists. The phantom hound is usually seen running towards Hollocombe. Most of these great spectral black hounds, of which there are stories all over the country, are linked to evil in some form or other: one paces in front of the phantom coach of the wicked Lady Howard at Okehampton, and others

The George and Dragon at Hatherleigh, where one of the ghosts is a welcome sight to the male clientele at this popular pub.

accompany the Devil across Dartmoor. This dog, however, has no such stories attached to it. It merely runs over the moor on misty days and foggy nights on some endless unexplained quest of its own.

OKEHAMPTON

The most spectacular phantom in Devon is to be found in Okehampton. This is the ghost of the wicked Lady Howard, accompanied by her spectral entourage.

According to local legend, the wicked Lady Howard was the evil daughter of an evil father. She married four times, each husband being murdered by her

The ruins of Okehampton castle, which is the starting point for the journey of Devon's most spectacular phantom – the coach of bones.

after the briefest of marriages. To atone for these crimes, the spirit of the guilty woman is doomed to sally forth from Okehampton Castle in her dreaded coach, until a certain task is completed. The coach, it is said, is made up of the bones of her victims, the supporting post at each corner being topped by a grinning skull. In front of the coach runs a huge black hound, which bays and howls in tones that alternate between mortal anguish and evil aggression. The coachman has no head and is reckoned to be the ghost of the servant who was decapitated by the wicked lady's father.

In this spectacular phantom coach, the shade of Lady Howard drives from Okehampton Castle to Fitzford House, near Tavistock. In the course of the journey, she or the dog must pick one blade of grass from the roadside. Only when the verges of the road have been entirely stripped of grass will the penance of the murderess be completed and the coach of bones cease terrorizing the good folk of Devon. In addition the wicked Lady Howard had the task of singling out those she felt sufficiently deep in sin to act as her servants through the time of her penance. When she encountered such folk, she would halt her coach and open the door for them to join her.

An old song used to be sung in Okehampton to commemorate their most famous spectral resident.

> My lady's coach hath nodding plumes
> The driver hath no head
> My lady is an ashen white
> Like one that is long dead.
> 'Now pray step in,' my lady saith,
> 'Now pray step in and ride.'
>
> I'd rather walk a hundred miles
> And run by night and day
> Than have that carriage halt for me
> And hear my lady say
> 'Now pray step in and make no din,
> Step in with me and ride.'
>
> 'There's room, I trow, by me for you
> And all the world beside.'

But Lady Howard is seen not only in her terrifying coach. She has also been seen walking around the ruins of Okehampton Castle. One day, in the 1970s, she was seen by two people at once; she was sitting by the gates to the castle, calmly combing her long dark hair.

The real life Lady Howard in question lived in Okehampton during the early 17th century. Her wicked father, John Fitze, had inherited a vast fortune from his merchant father. Like many men of his day, Fitze felt that trade was rather beneath his dignity; so he sold his father's various business interests and spent the money on the more gentlemanly investment of land. To make doubly certain that his new status would accord with the dignity he felt was his due, John Fitze bought only freehold land – or thought he did. Under the complex land laws of the time, freehold land meant that Fitze would owe taxes, duties, and rents to the king only and to no other person.

Unfortunately, Fitze made a mistake. One piece of land he bought carried with it the duty of contributing towards the upkeep of the bridge over the Okement River in Okehampton. The day came when the bridge needed repairing and Mr Slanning, the man whose lands entailed organising the repair work, rode over to ask Fitze for his contribution. As luck would have it, Fitze was holding a hard drinking dinner for some of his friends and had just been boasting that he held land free of all dues. When Slanning arrived to collect the money, Fitze took this as a personal insult, and in a drunken rage he stabbed him through the heart.

The guests fled, leaving Fitze alone in Fitzford House. He became convinced that the local law officers would be calling on him. At dawn there was a loud hammering on his door. In a fright, Fitze drew his sword, opened the door, and sliced off the head of the man standing outside. This turned out to be his own servant, whom he had ordered to rouse him early so that he could attend to some business, despite his expected hangover. A few hours later, the local magistrate did arrive to arrest Fitze, but found only his body. According to the cook, Fitze had killed himself on recognising the headless corpse of his servant.

So much for the wicked father, but what of the wicked Lady Howard herself? Mary Fitze was only nine years old when her father killed himself, and her care passed to the king. But James I handed control over to the Earl of Northumberland, although he had no links to the Fitze family and the move ignored the wishes of the girl's cousins in Devon. Northumberland at once started felling timber on the Fitze estates, and two years later he married Mary to his brother, Sir Alan Percy.

Sir Alan died three years later, but, before Northumberland could find her another husband, 16-year-old Mary ran off with Thomas Darcy, who three years after the marriage inherited the title Earl of Rivers. Two years later Rivers

*The White Hart Hotel stands in the centre of Okehampton
and is haunted by two ghosts.*

died, and Mary, now having made herself full mistress of her estates and her destiny, married Sir Charles Howard, a younger brother of the Earl of Suffolk. Thus it was as Lady Howard that she came home to Devon. This marriage did not last much longer than the previous two, and by 1622 Lady Howard was a widow once again.

As her fourth husband she chose Sir Richard Grenville. He was a grandson of the Richard Grenville who had fought alongside Sir Francis Drake against the Spanish Armada and had died a hero's death when his lone warship was attacked by a fleet of 94 Spanish galleons. Lady Howard's new husband, however did not take after his illustrious grandfather, but was a womanising wastrel. Fortunately for Lady Howard, he died within months of the marriage, leaving his own spreading estates to be added to those of his wife.

It was probably this last death that led to local rumours alleging that the Lady had done away with an inconvenient husband, but nothing was ever proved, and she retained her greatly enlarged estates, passing them on to the children from her marriage to Sir Charles Howard.

Compared with the colourful wicked lady the other ghosts of Okehampton are a tame collection. The High Street is haunted by a ghostly horseman who rides at breakneck speed down from the hills west of the town to the door of the church, and then vanishes. From the cut of his clothes, he is usually thought to be a Cavalier but nobody seems to know any more about him than that.

The White Hart Hotel has two phantoms. The first is an elderly female dressed in a long black dress or cloak. She is seen downstairs, often in the main bar or near the staircase, and she is blamed for the fact that frequently small items in the bar or office go missing, only to turn up a few days later in an unexpected place. On occasion glasses and ashtrays have flown around the bar, as if thrown by unseen hands. Again, the old lady gets the blame.

The hotel's other phantom is altogether different. This is a small boy dressed in the sort of quaint sailor suit favoured for small boys in the late Victorian and Edwardian eras. He is seen running around the upper landings in a distraught manner, crying plaintively for his mother. Some guests who have encountered this spectre have phoned down to reception to alert them to the problem. The records of the White Hart are well kept but record no incident from the relevant period that could account for this ghost. No boy has died here, nor was one abandoned by his mother. It is a mystery.

Very well documented, however, is the career of Benjamin Geare, whose ghost lurks round Okement River, a short distance upstream of Okehampton. Geare managed to be elected mayor of Okehampton four times during the 1670s, as much because of his popularity as a local character as for his administrative abilities. The good townsfolk referred to Geare as Bingie, and often hailed him when they passed. After his death, his ghost was soon seen flitting about Cranmere Pool, a small lake formed by the Okement River south of the town. The reason why Bingie Geare should favour this spot has been forgotten in the course of time.

LAPFORD

Lapford is a small tranquil village which shows a welcoming face to visitors, but it has not always been so quiet. Take January 1181, for instance. A troop of armed knights rode into the village carrying an arrest warrant signed by the king himself. The knights wanted Sir William de Tracy, the lord of the manor of Lapford and owner of extensive estates in the area.

Tracy's crime was to have murdered the Archbishop of Canterbury, Thomas à Becket, in Canterbury cathedral on the night of 29th December. At the time Becket was engaged in a long and bitter quarrel with Henry II about the respective rights and duties of royal government and the Church. By killing Becket, Tracy and his three henchmen hoped to win the favour of the king. All they got was the enmity of the Church.

Tracy was excused execution as he pleaded that he thought the king had ordered the killing. The king, however, maintained that his words had been spoken in a fit of anger and that he had not really meant them. Henry had to accept the Church's rulings and end the dispute. Tracy, meanwhile, was ordered to build new churches on his estates and to endow various ecclesiastical establishments.

At Lapford, Tracy's rebuilding began in 1180 and was not complete at the time of his death, when the work stopped. The nave was largely untouched, but Tracy did complete the chancel, tower, and porch. Just before his death, Tracy had the church rededicated to St Thomas à Becket, the murdered archbishop who had been canonised in 1183. The north aisle was added in around 1300 and the nave rebuilt in the 15th century, producing the church that stands today.

Lapford church was granted the right of sanctuary. This meant that any criminal who managed to reach the church door and grab the knocker was exempt from the king's justice, and could claim to be tried by the Church instead. Typically, the Church chose not to spill blood and so the criminal would be spared execution, nose slitting, or any of the other more brutal punishments of medieval justice. Instead, he would be given penances to carry out or fines to pay. The knocker installed by William de Tracy still graces the main door, and the ghost of the knight has been seen moving around the church. He appears in a full mail coat, the typical armour of his time, and usually seems to be deep in thought.

Very different is the ghost of St Thomas à Becket. This spectre gallops up to the church door mounted on a ferocious black steed, pauses a few seconds, and then turns and gallops off towards Nymet. For some reason, Becket's ghost appears most frequently on 27th December, though the murder took place on 29th December.

Another killing has left its spectral mark on Lapford. This murder took place during the reign of William IV, between 1830 and 1837. The victim was the curate of St Thomas's, and the man arrested for the crime was none other than the vicar, the Revd John Arundel Radford. As might be expected, the crime and subsequent trial caused an absolute sensation throughout the county. It was thought that the curate may have become a bit too familiar with the vicar's wife, Thomasina Radford, and spurred the vicar into a jealous rage. The evidence that came out at the trial seemed damning.

When the verdict came it was a surprise. Radford was found not guilty. This was not, the jury foreman said, because they thought him innocent but because 'We haven't hanged a parson here yet, and we're not going to start now'. Radford returned to his parish and continued as rector until his death in 1867.

As he lay dying, Radford asked that he should be buried in the chancel of the church that he had served for 42 years and that four different ancestors of his had also served as rectors. Mindful of the likely crime the man had committed, however, the bishop refused, and Radford was buried outside the door, his much loved wife joining him soon after.

Radford was not happy. Shortly after his burial, the cross on his grave shifted to one side. It was restored, but slipped again. Then the ghost of the rector was seen hovering nearby. Somehow nobody felt like setting the gravestone straight again. The ghostly rector has been seen from time to time ever since. He is usually witnessed either sorrowfully staring at his gravestone or wandering the streets of his former parish.

INDEX